FEB

12/09-9

P9-CEN-337

Abraham Lincoln

written by
Joe Dunn

illustrated by
Rod Espinosa

GLEN ELLYN PUBLIC LIBRARY
400 DUANE STREET
GLEN ELLYN, ILLINOIS 60137

magic
Wagon

visit us at
www.abdopublishing.com

Published by Magic Wagon, a division of the ABDO Publishing Group, 8000 West 78th Street, Edina, Minnesota 55439. Copyright © 2008 by Abdo Consulting Group, Inc. International copyrights reserved in all countries. All rights reserved. No part of this book may be reproduced in any form without written permission from the publisher. Graphic Planet™ is a trademark and logo of Magic Wagon.

Printed in the United States.

Written by Joe Dunn
Illustrated by Rod Espinosa
Colored and lettered by Rod Espinosa
Edited by Stephanie Hedlund
Interior layout and design by Antarctic Press
Cover art by Rod Espinosa
Cover design by Neil Klinepier

Library of Congress Cataloging-in-Publication Data

Dunn, Joeming W.
    Abraham Lincoln / written by Joe Dunn ; illustrated by Rod Espinosa.
    p. cm. -- (Bio-graphics)
    Includes bibliographical references and index.
    ISBN 978-1-60270-064-2
    1. Lincoln, Abraham, 1809-1865--Juvenile literature. 2. Presidents--United States--Biography--Juvenile literature. 3. Graphic novels. I. Espinosa, Rod. II. Title.

E457.905.D86 2008
 973.7092--dc22
 [B]   2007006437

TABLE of CONTENTS

He is one of the greatest presidents of the United States of America.
He presided over one of the most difficult times in American history.
Under his term, slaves were freed, and the union of states preserved.
He is the great emancipator.
He is Abraham Lincoln!

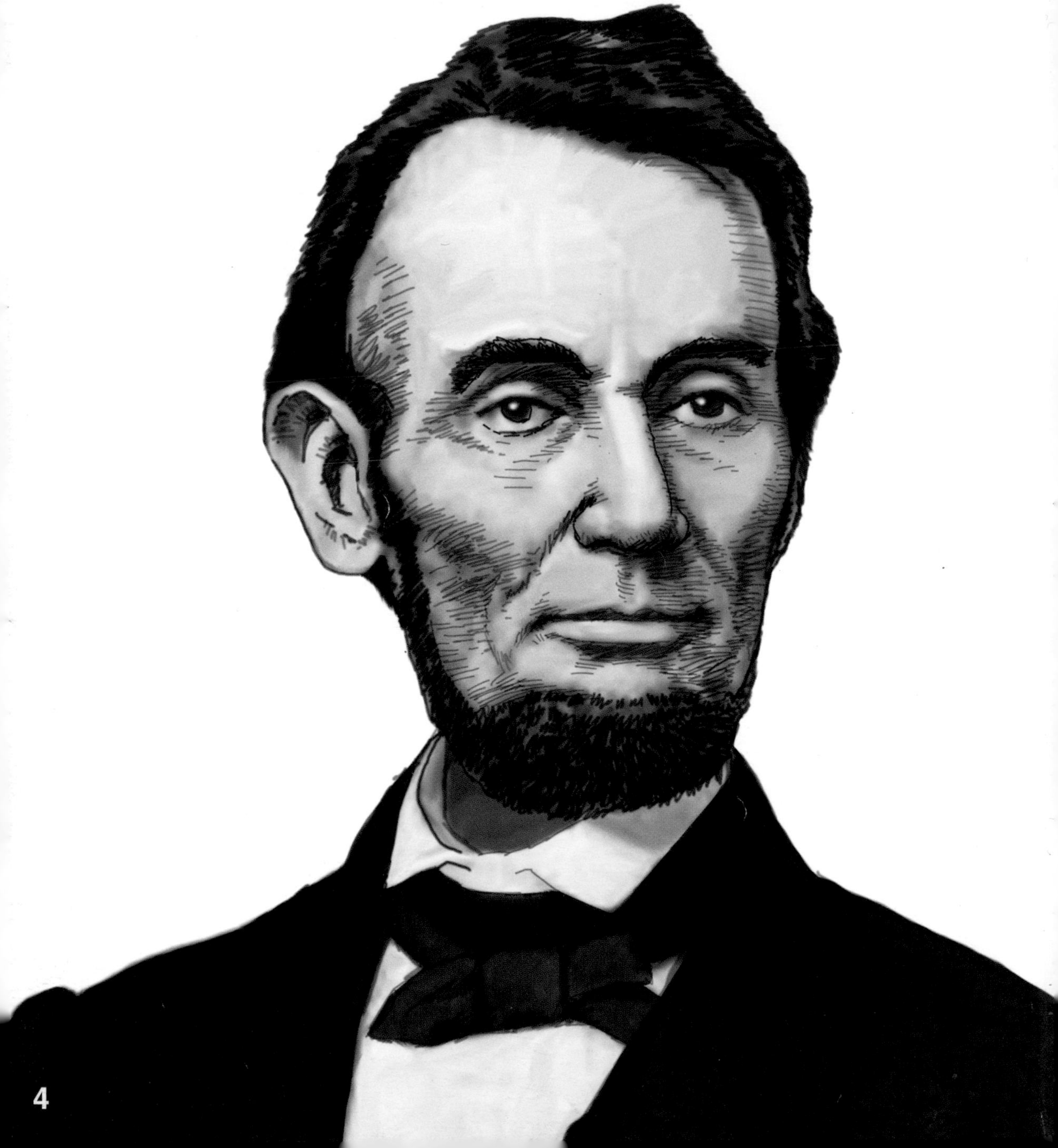

Chapter 1 A Humble Birth

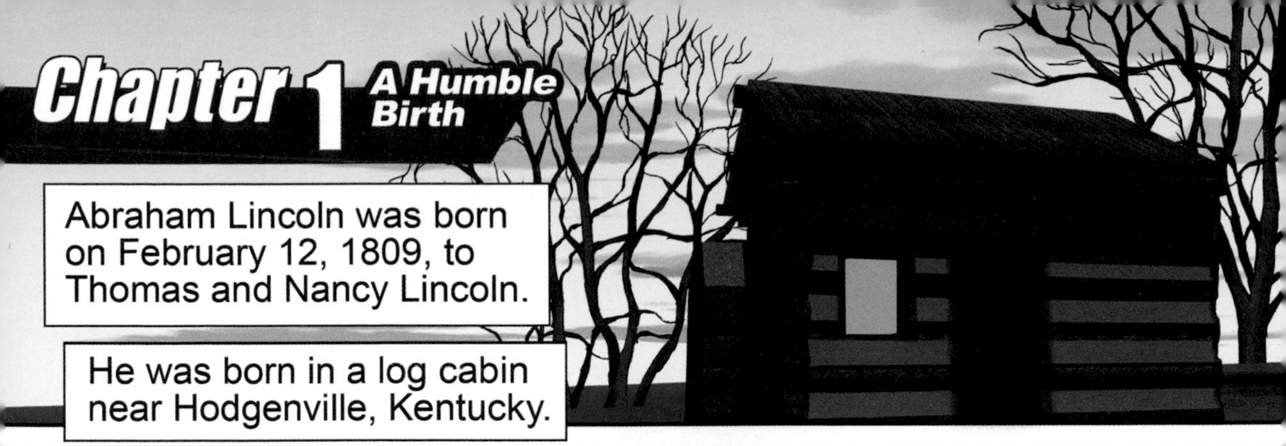

Abraham Lincoln was born on February 12, 1809, to Thomas and Nancy Lincoln.
He was born in a log cabin near Hodgenville, Kentucky.

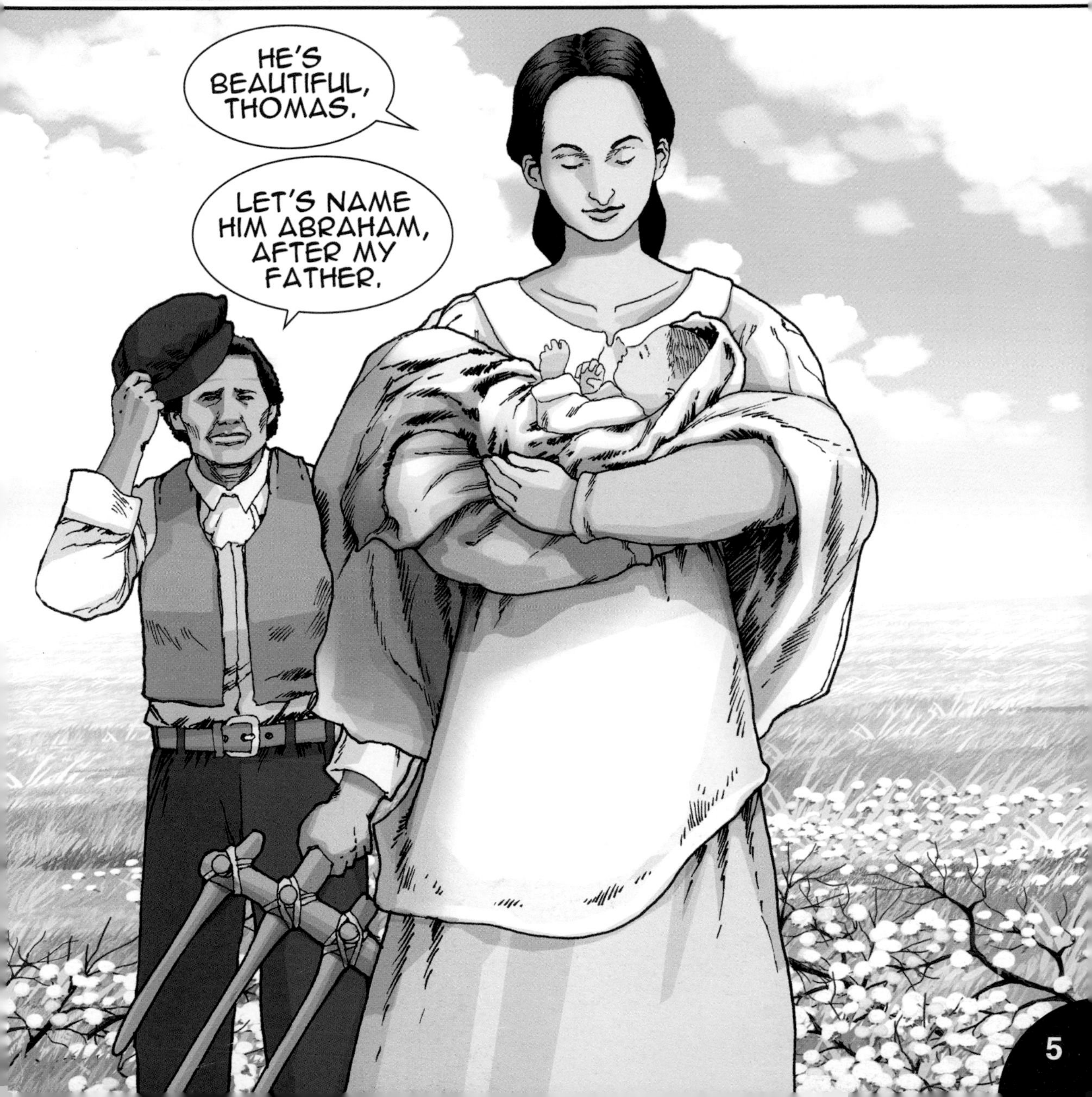

HE'S BEAUTIFUL, THOMAS.
LET'S NAME HIM ABRAHAM, AFTER MY FATHER.

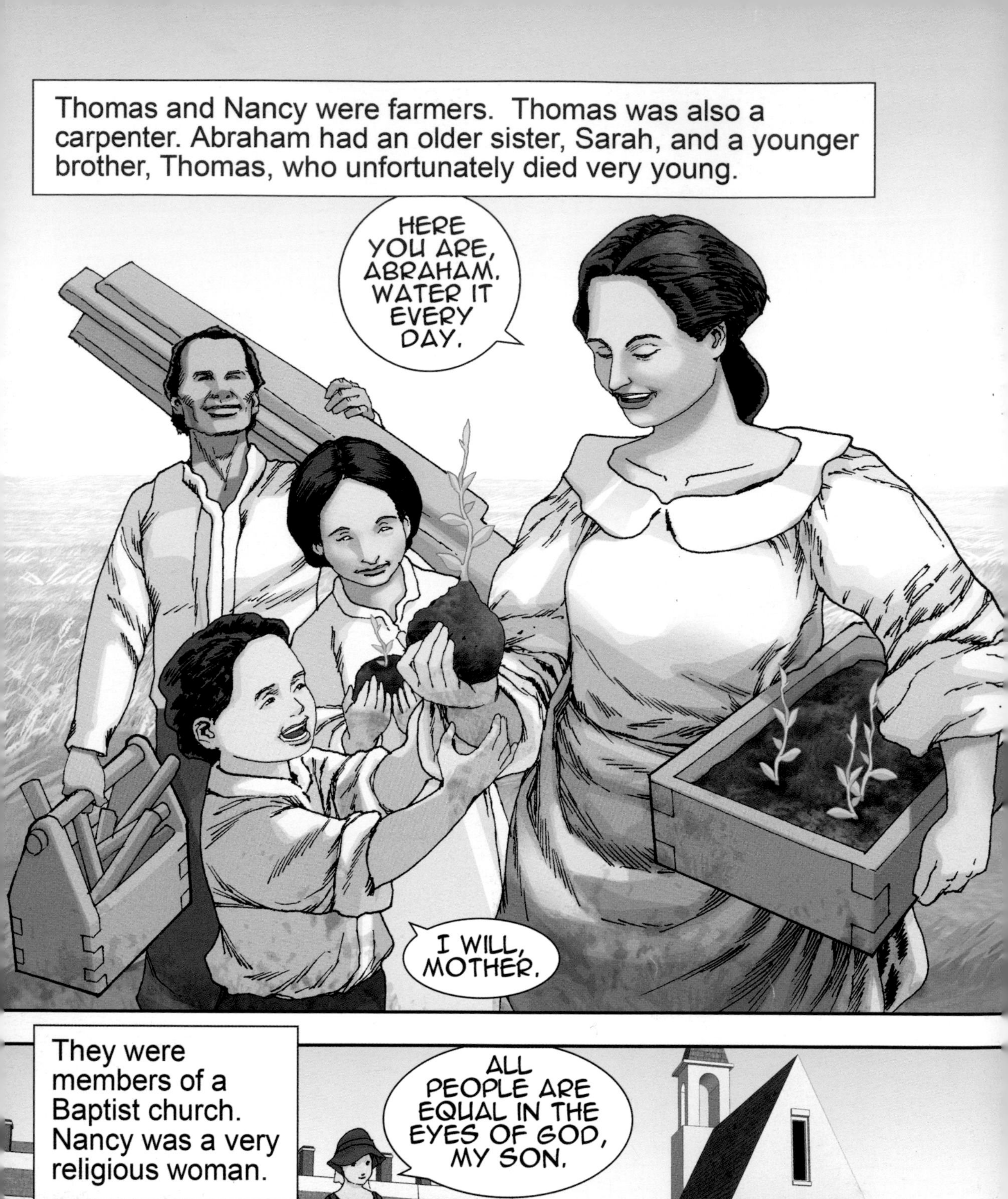
Thomas and Nancy were farmers. Thomas was also a carpenter. Abraham had an older sister, Sarah, and a younger brother, Thomas, who unfortunately died very young.
HERE YOU ARE, ABRAHAM. WATER IT EVERY DAY.
I WILL, MOTHER.

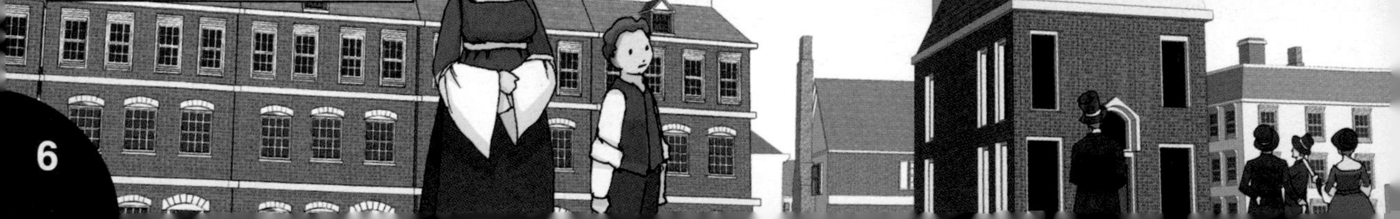
They were members of a Baptist church. Nancy was a very religious woman.
ALL PEOPLE ARE EQUAL IN THE EYES OF GOD, MY SON.

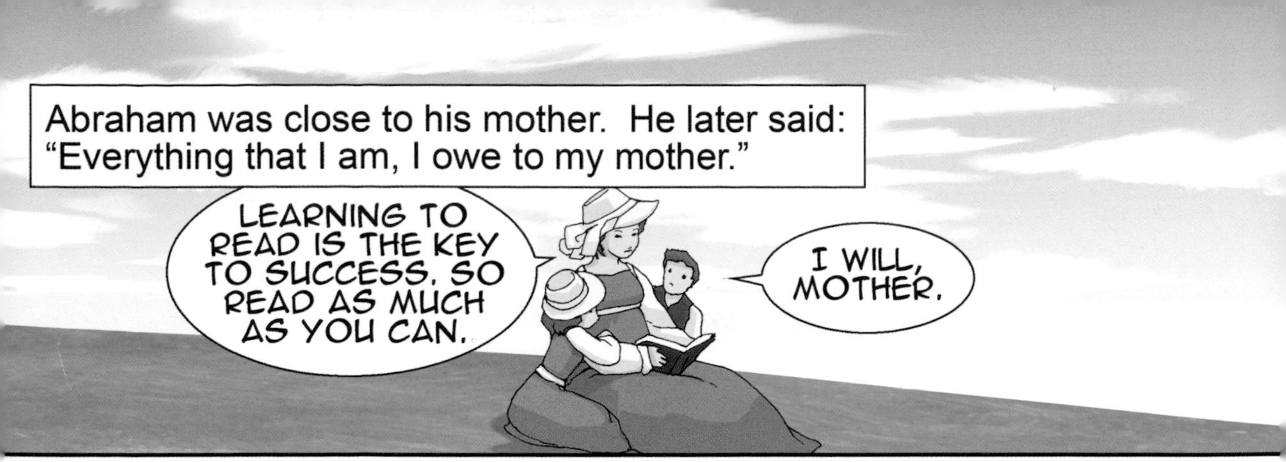
Abraham was close to his mother. He later said: "Everything that I am, I owe to my mother."
LEARNING TO READ IS THE KEY TO SUCCESS. SO READ AS MUCH AS YOU CAN.
I WILL, MOTHER.

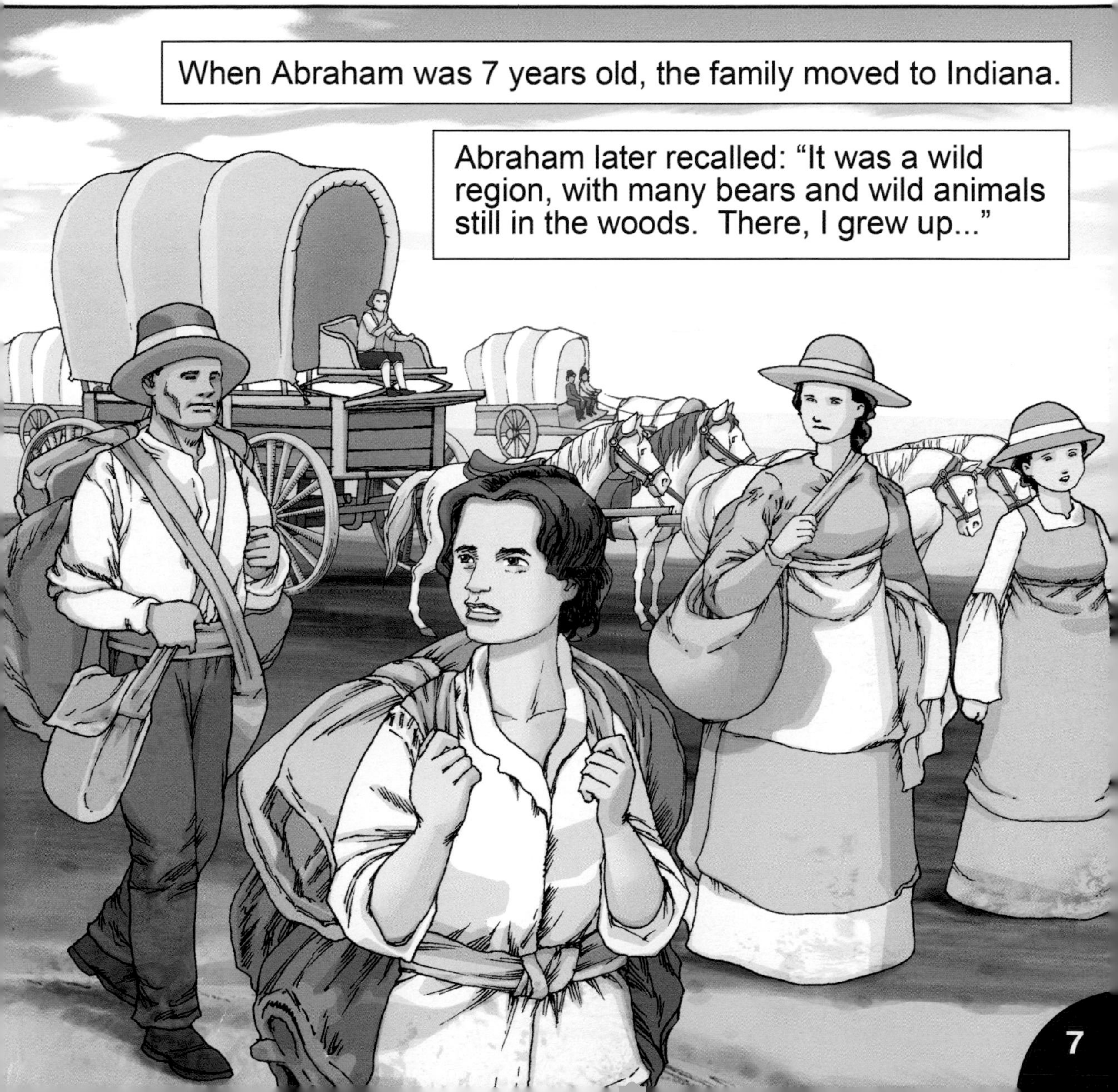
When Abraham was 7 years old, the family moved to Indiana.
Abraham later recalled: "It was a wild region, with many bears and wild animals still in the woods. There, I grew up..."

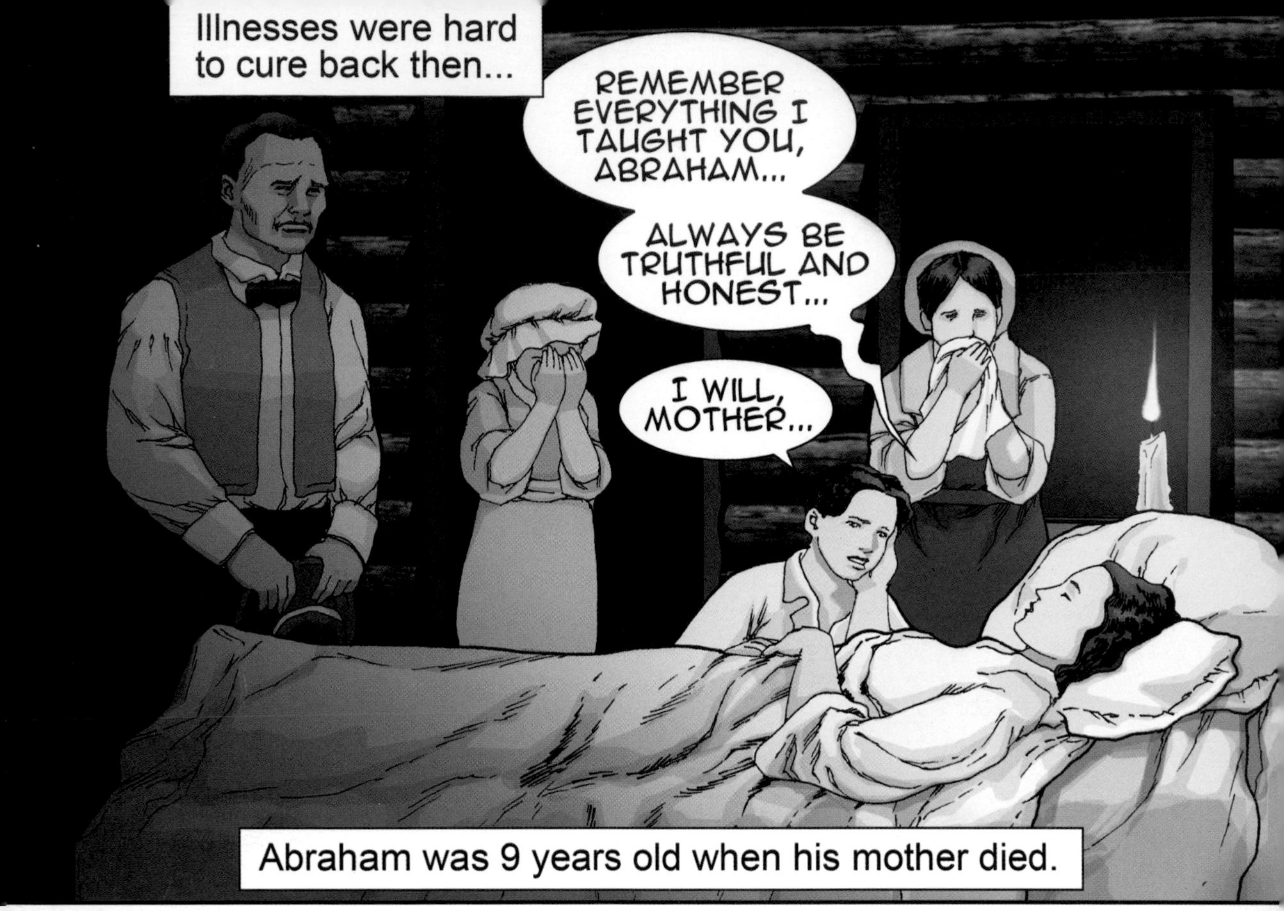
Illnesses were hard to cure back then...
REMEMBER EVERYTHING I TAUGHT YOU, ABRAHAM...
ALWAYS BE TRUTHFUL AND HONEST...
I WILL, MOTHER...
Abraham was 9 years old when his mother died.

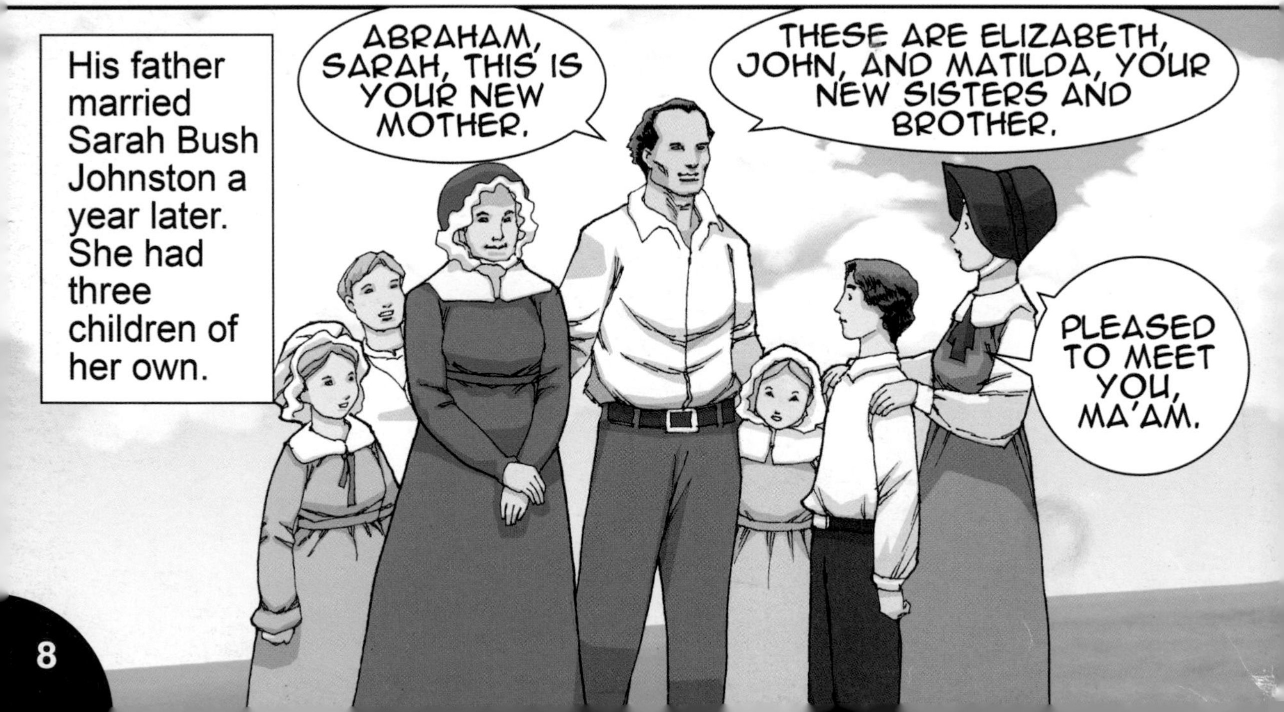
His father married Sarah Bush Johnston a year later. She had three children of her own.
ABRAHAM, SARAH, THIS IS YOUR NEW MOTHER.
THESE ARE ELIZABETH, JOHN, AND MATILDA, YOUR NEW SISTERS AND BROTHER.
PLEASED TO MEET YOU, MA'AM.

Chapter 2 A Passion for Reading

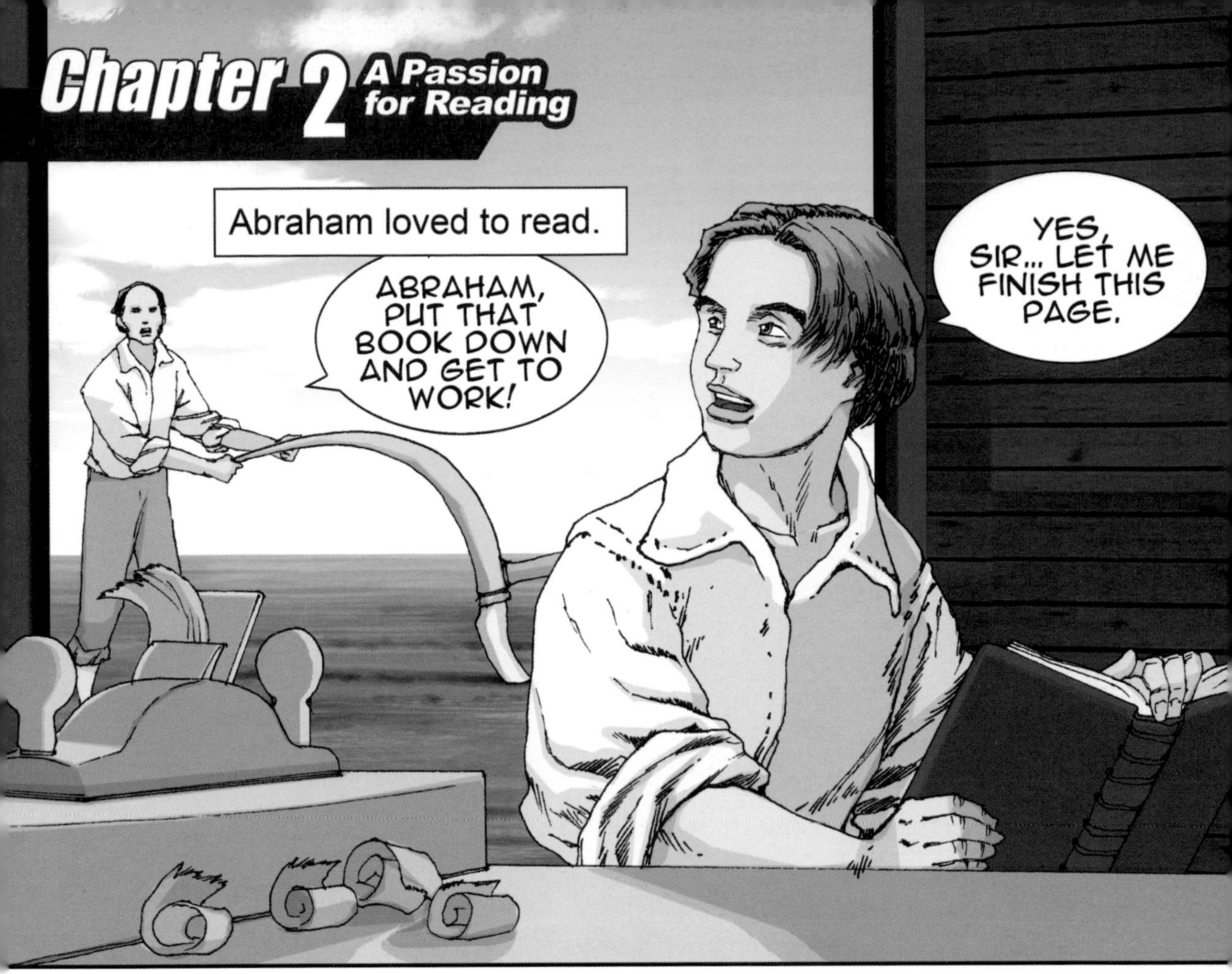
Abraham loved to read.
ABRAHAM, PUT THAT BOOK DOWN AND GET TO WORK!
YES, SIR... LET ME FINISH THIS PAGE.

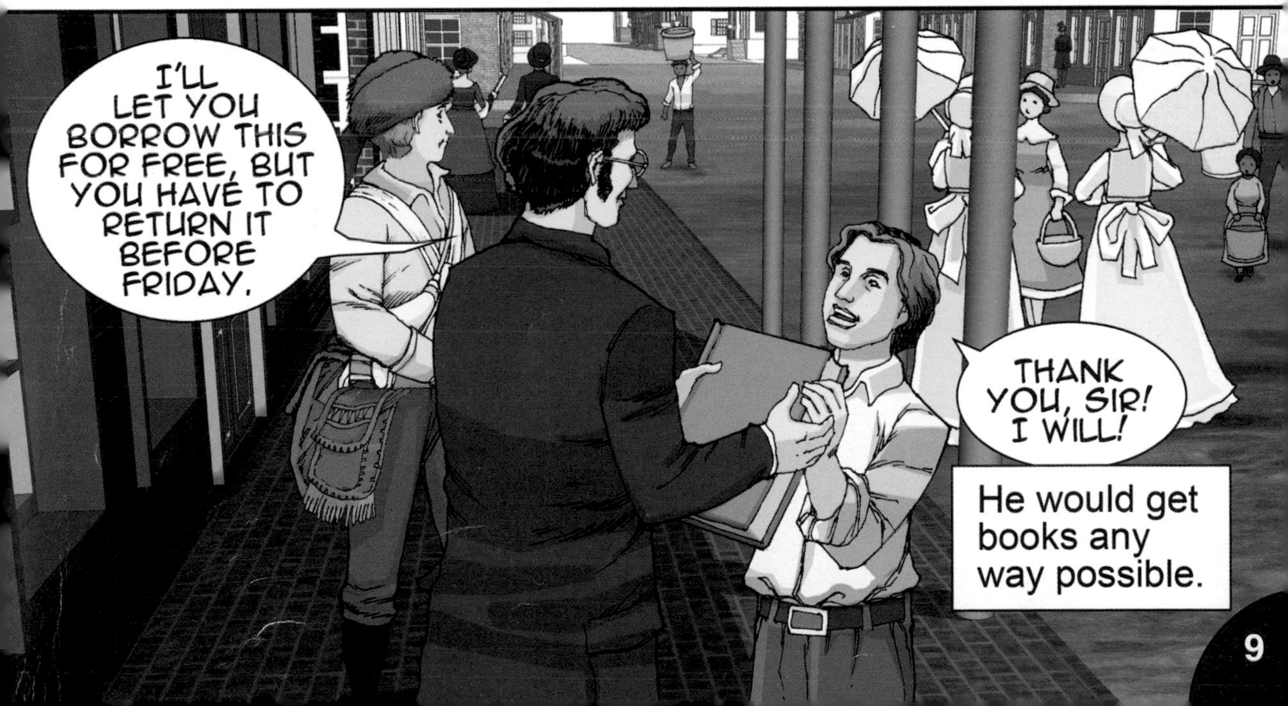
I'LL LET YOU BORROW THIS FOR FREE, BUT YOU HAVE TO RETURN IT BEFORE FRIDAY.
THANK YOU, SIR! I WILL!
He would get books any way possible.

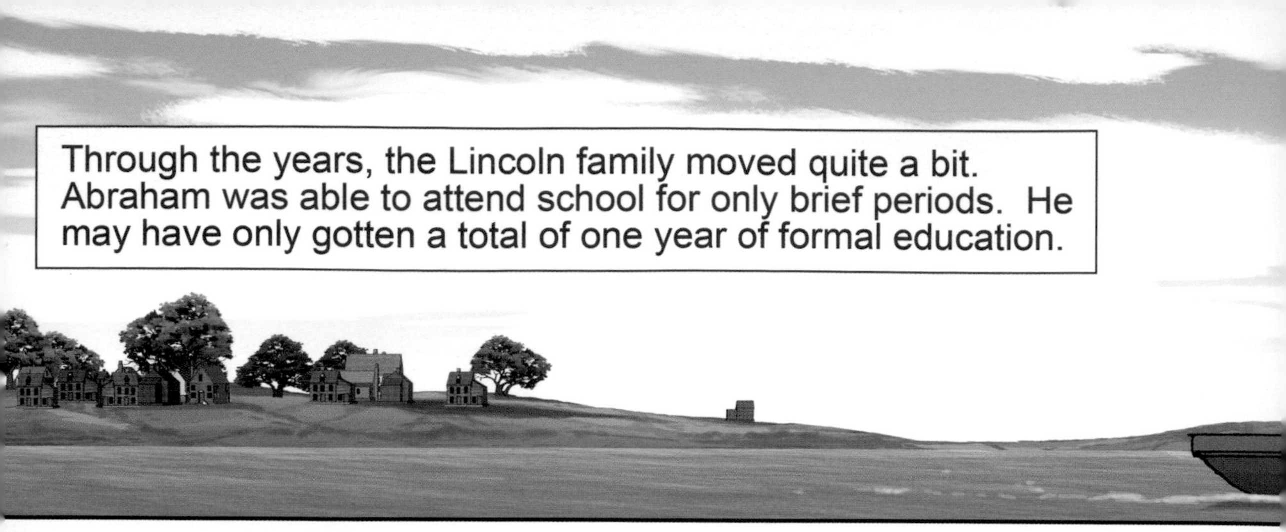
Through the years, the Lincoln family moved quite a bit. Abraham was able to attend school for only brief periods. He may have only gotten a total of one year of formal education.

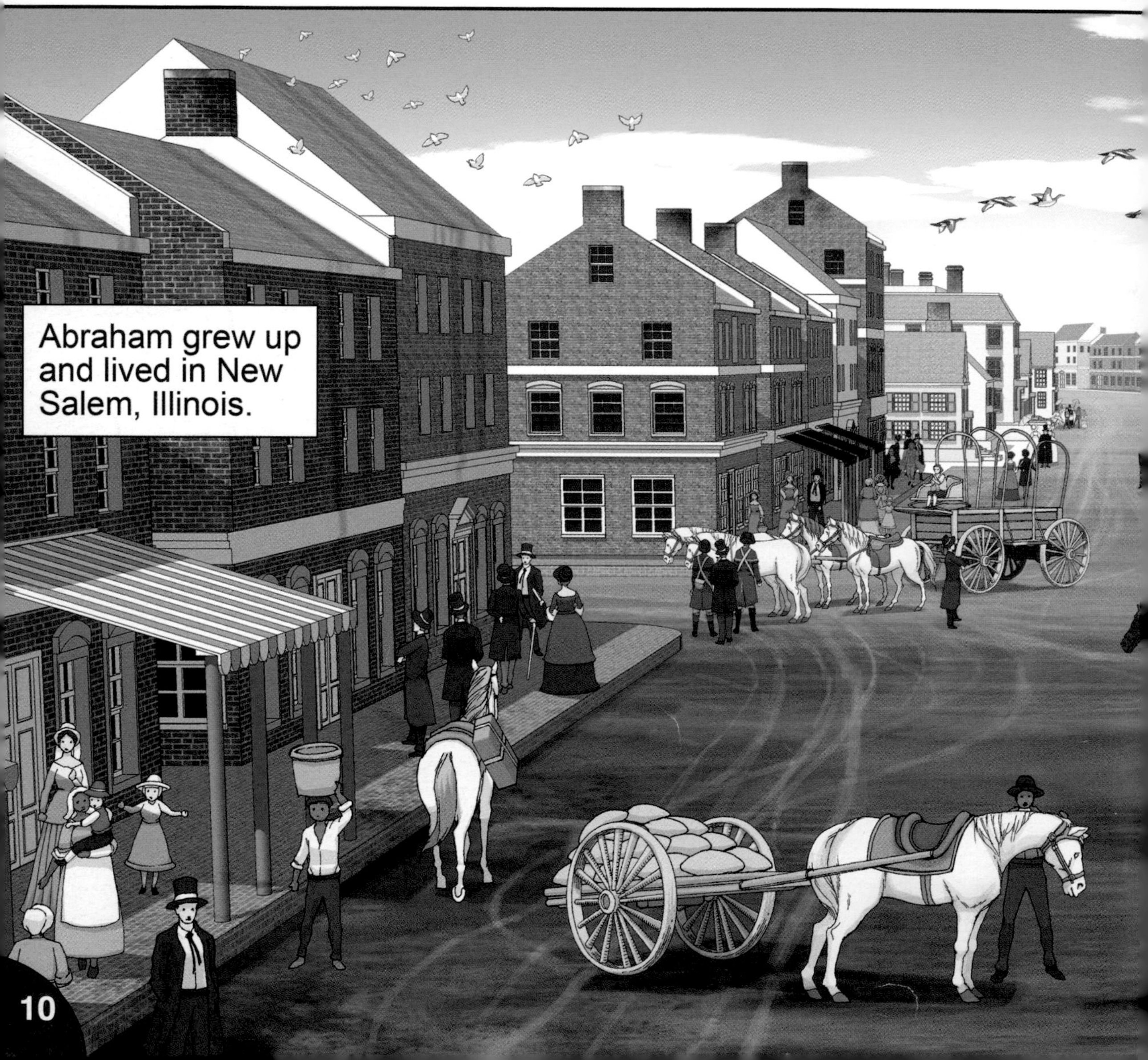
Abraham grew up and lived in New Salem, Illinois.

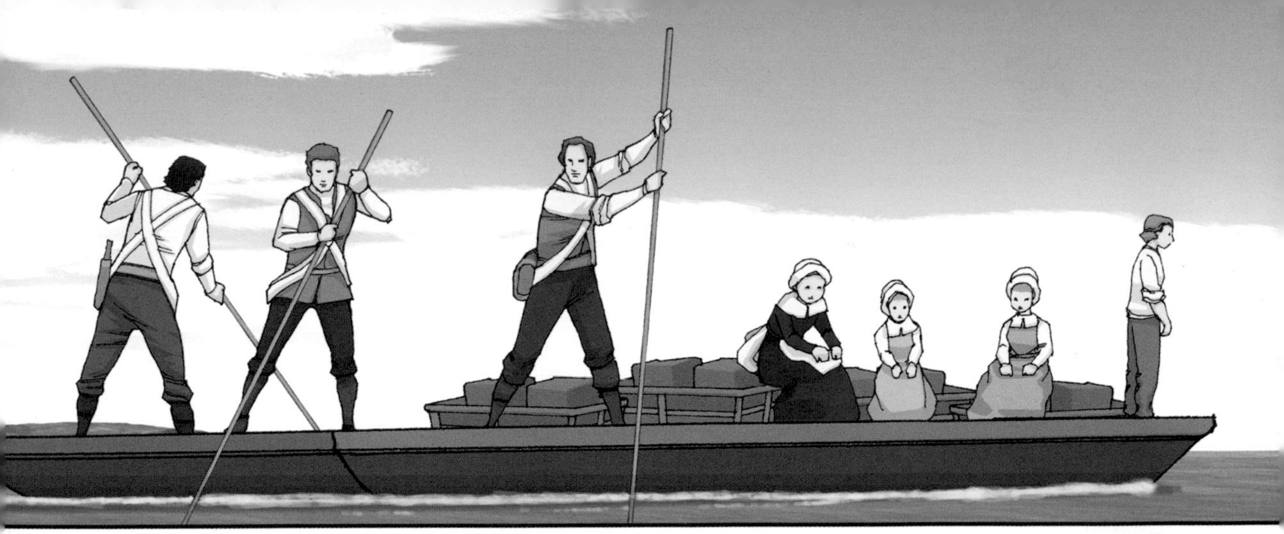

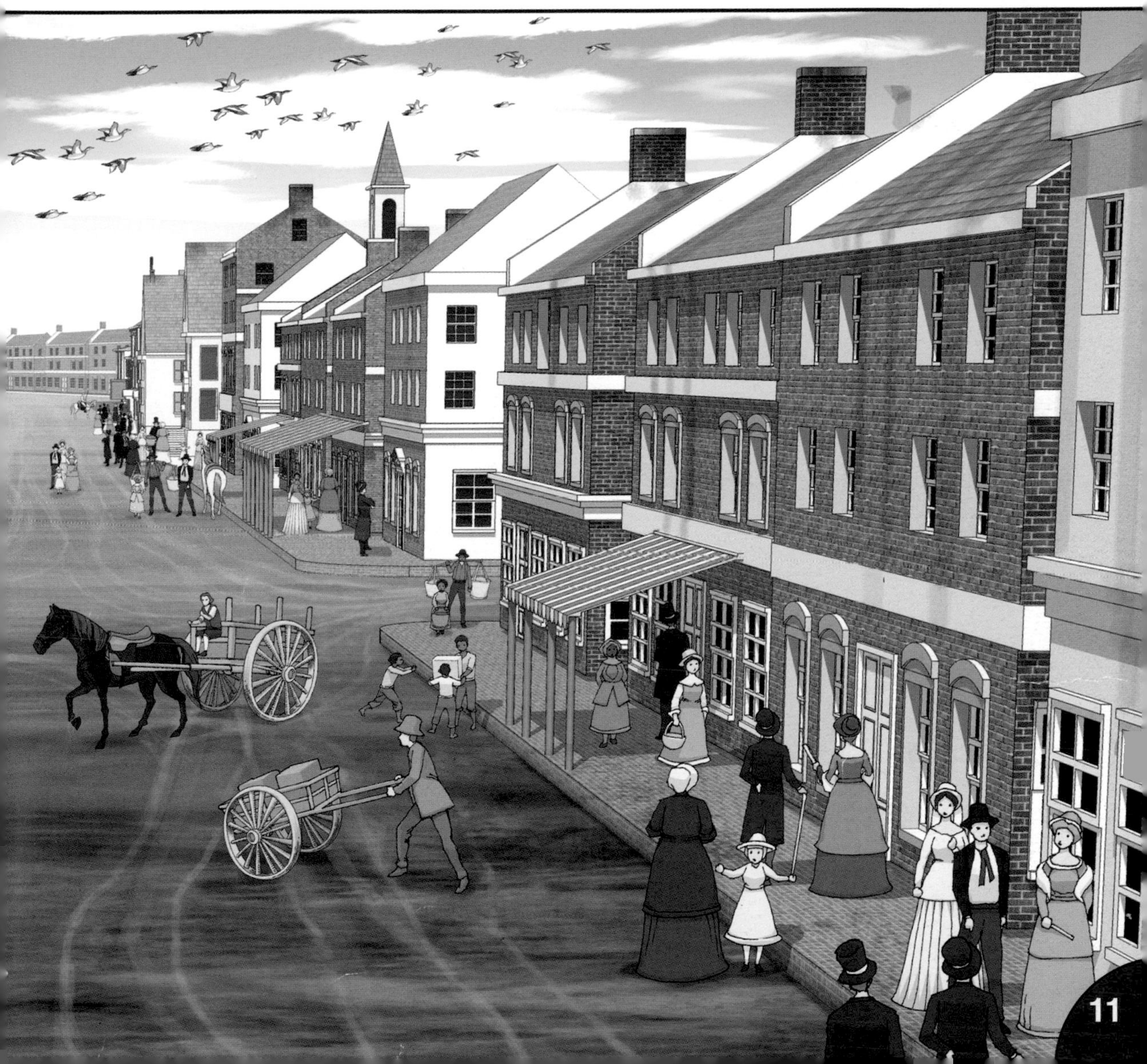

Chapter 3 Honest Abe

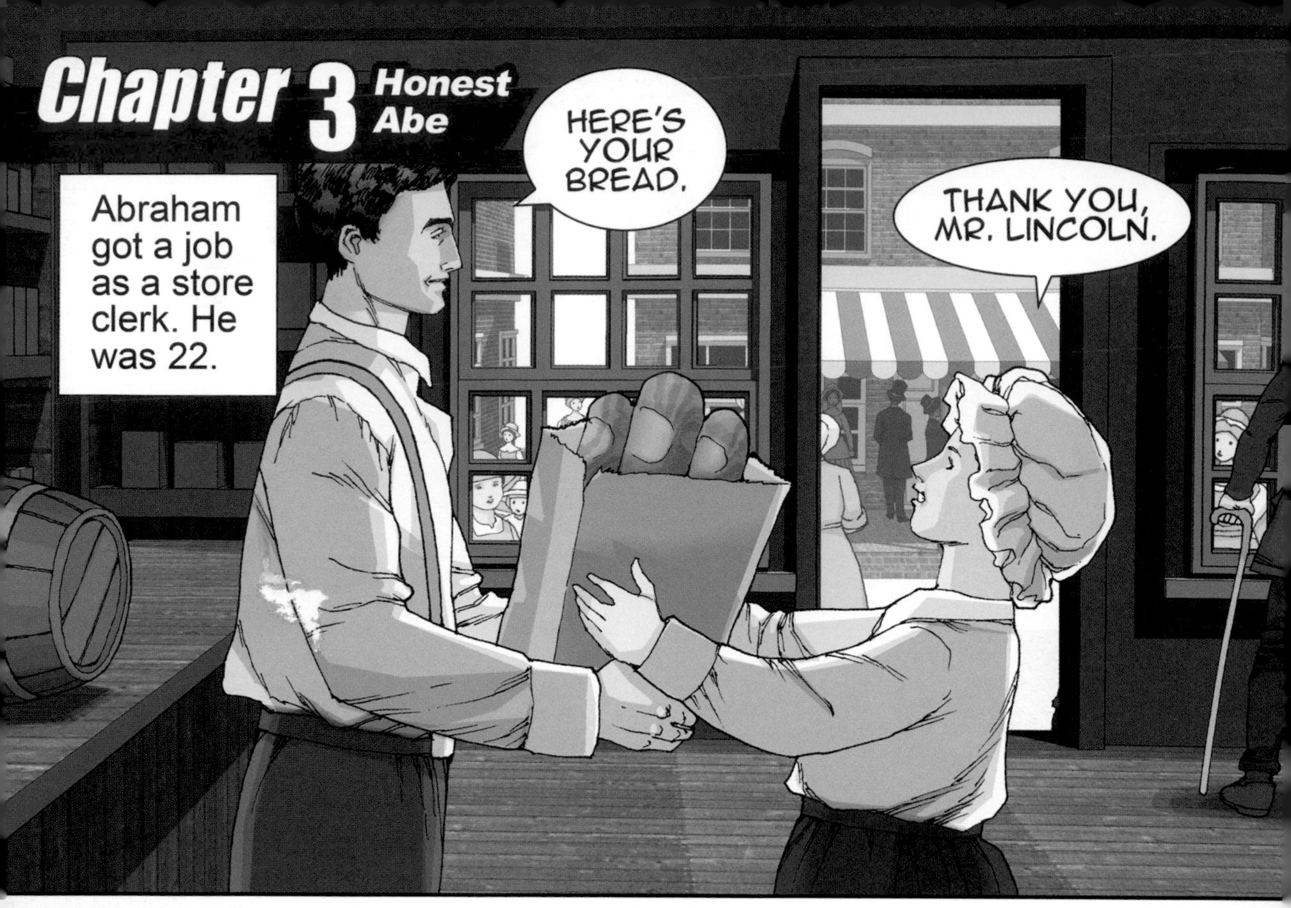
Abraham got a job as a store clerk. He was 22.
HERE'S YOUR BREAD.
THANK YOU, MR. LINCOLN.

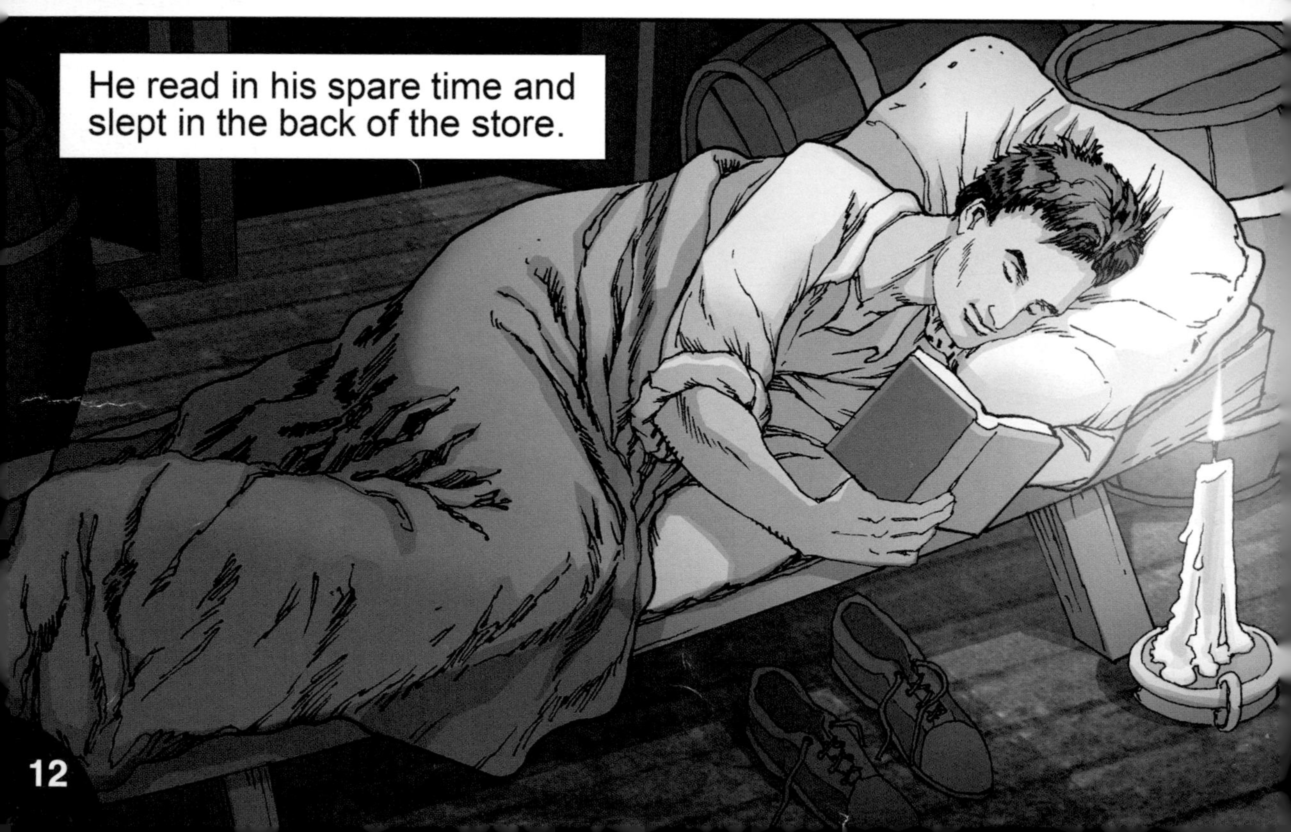
He read in his spare time and slept in the back of the store.

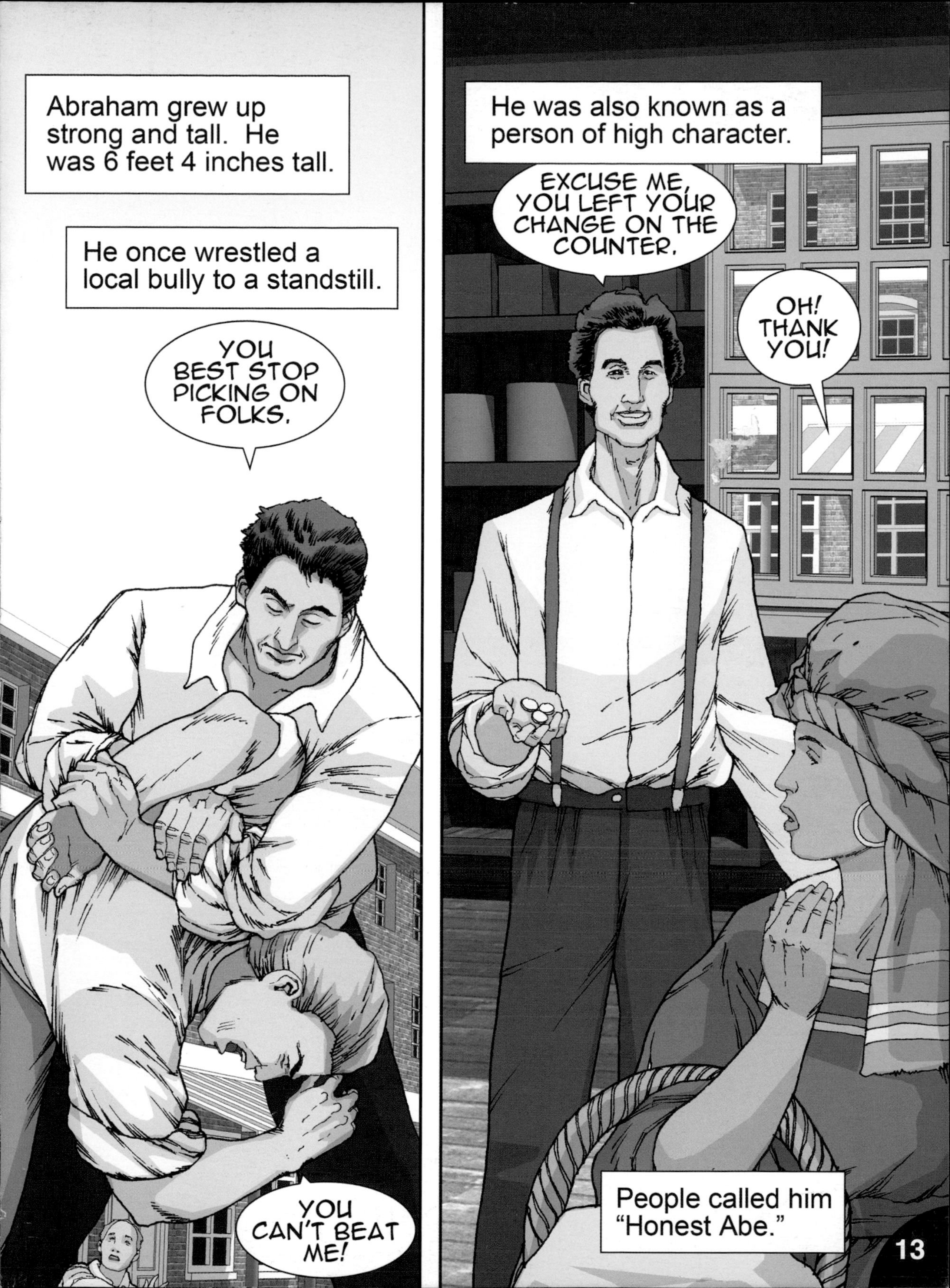
Abraham grew up strong and tall. He was 6 feet 4 inches tall.
He once wrestled a local bully to a standstill.
YOU BEST STOP PICKING ON FOLKS.
YOU CAN'T BEAT ME!
He was also known as a person of high character.
EXCUSE ME, YOU LEFT YOUR CHANGE ON THE COUNTER.
OH! THANK YOU!
People called him "Honest Abe."

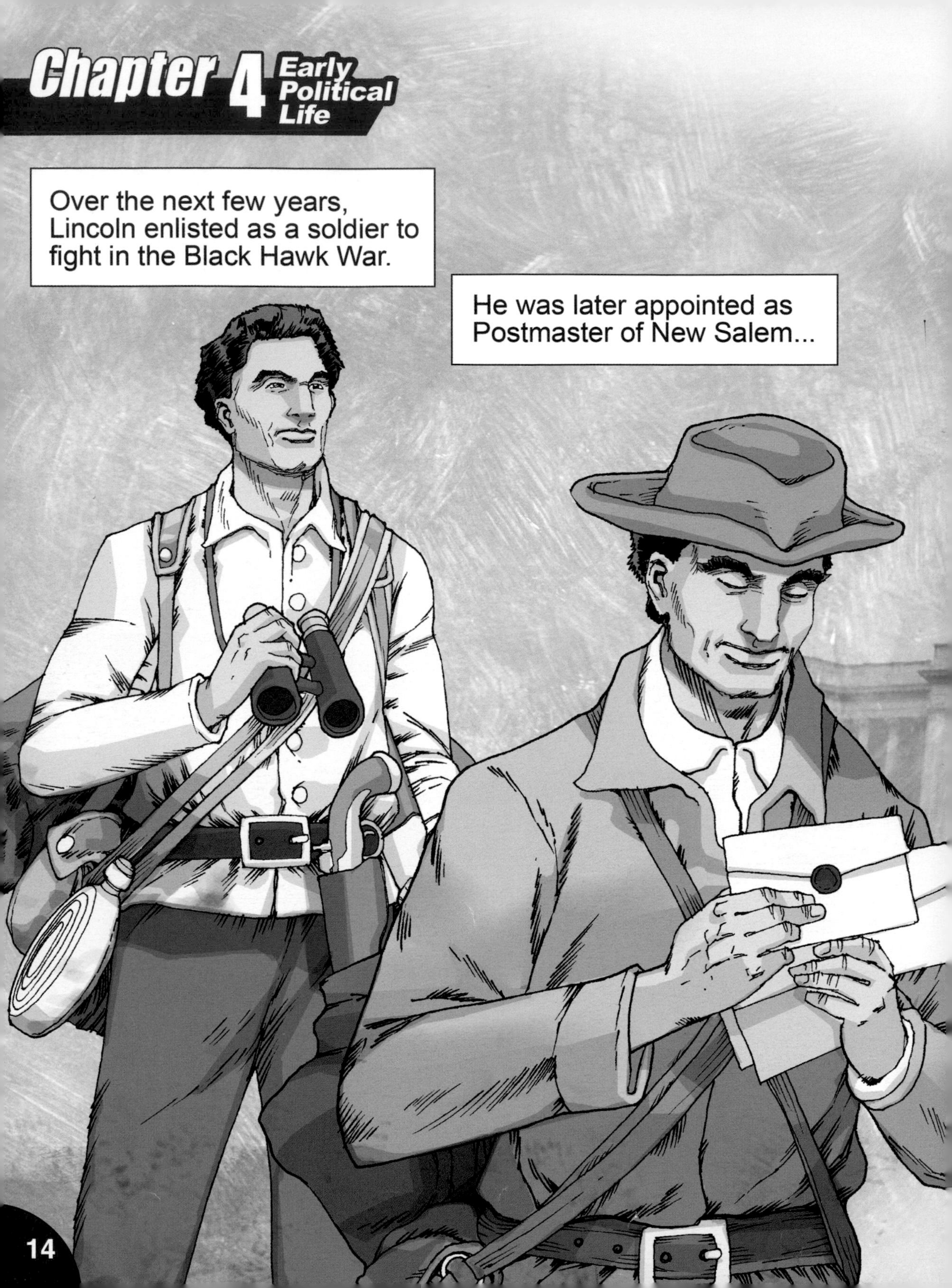

Chapter 4 Early Political Life
Over the next few years, Lincoln enlisted as a soldier to fight in the Black Hawk War.
He was later appointed as Postmaster of New Salem...

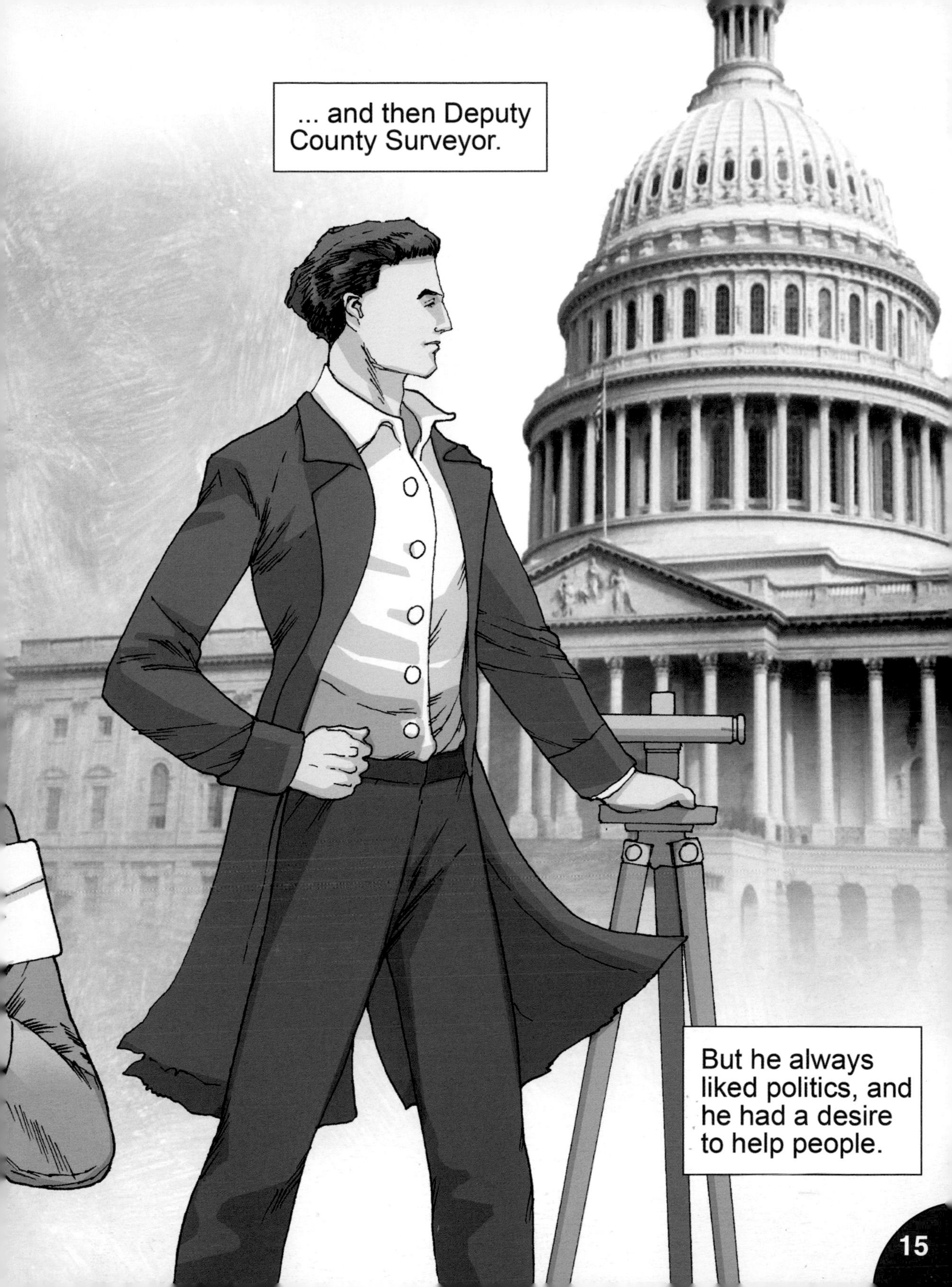
... and then Deputy County Surveyor.
But he always liked politics, and he had a desire to help people.

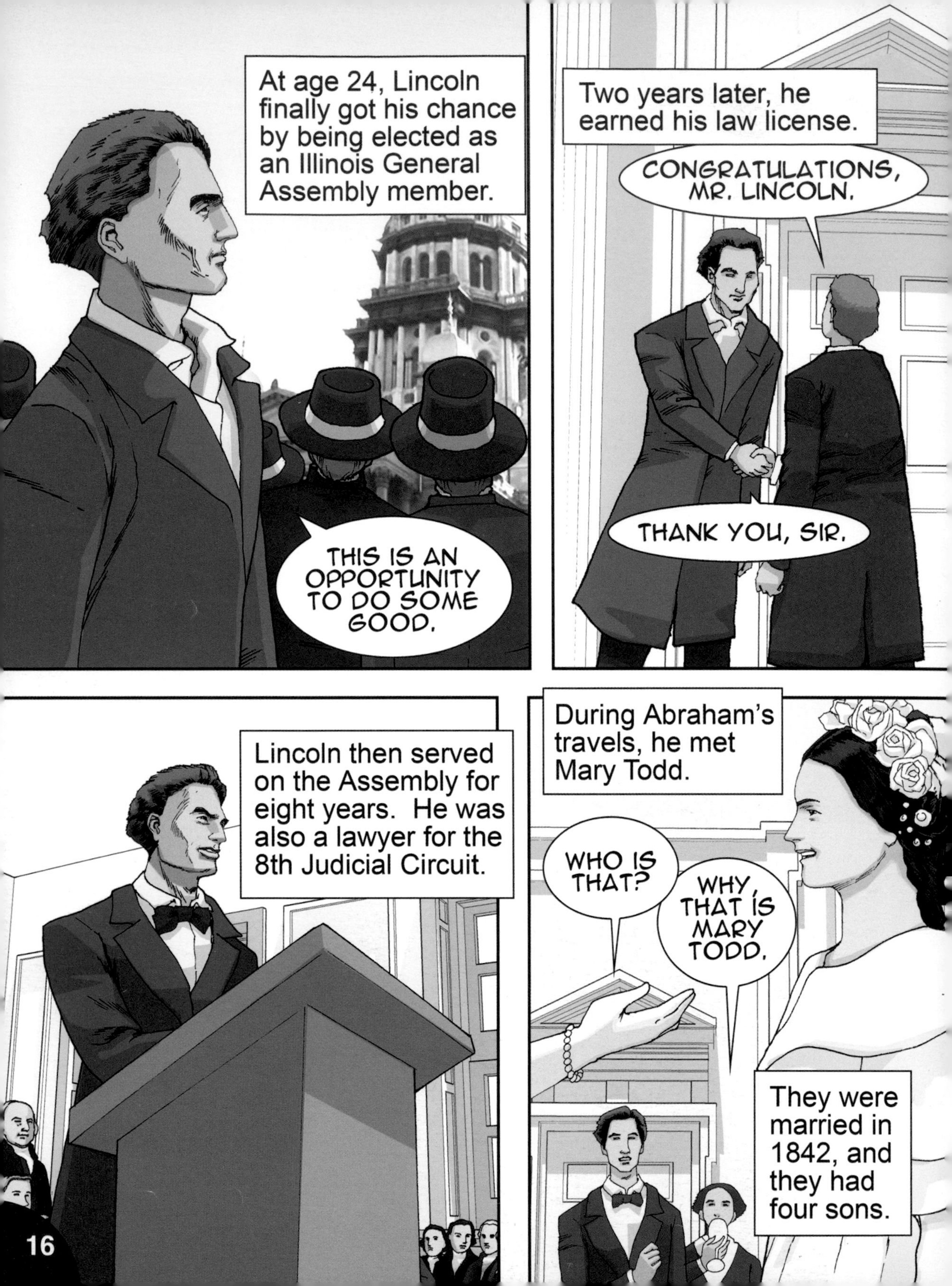

At age 24, Lincoln finally got his chance by being elected as an Illinois General Assembly member.
THIS IS AN OPPORTUNITY TO DO SOME GOOD.
Two years later, he earned his law license.
CONGRATULATIONS, MR. LINCOLN.
THANK YOU, SIR.
Lincoln then served on the Assembly for eight years. He was also a lawyer for the 8th Judicial Circuit.
During Abraham's travels, he met Mary Todd.
WHO IS THAT?
WHY, THAT IS MARY TODD.
They were married in 1842, and they had four sons.

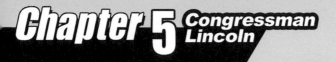

Chapter 5 Congressman Lincoln

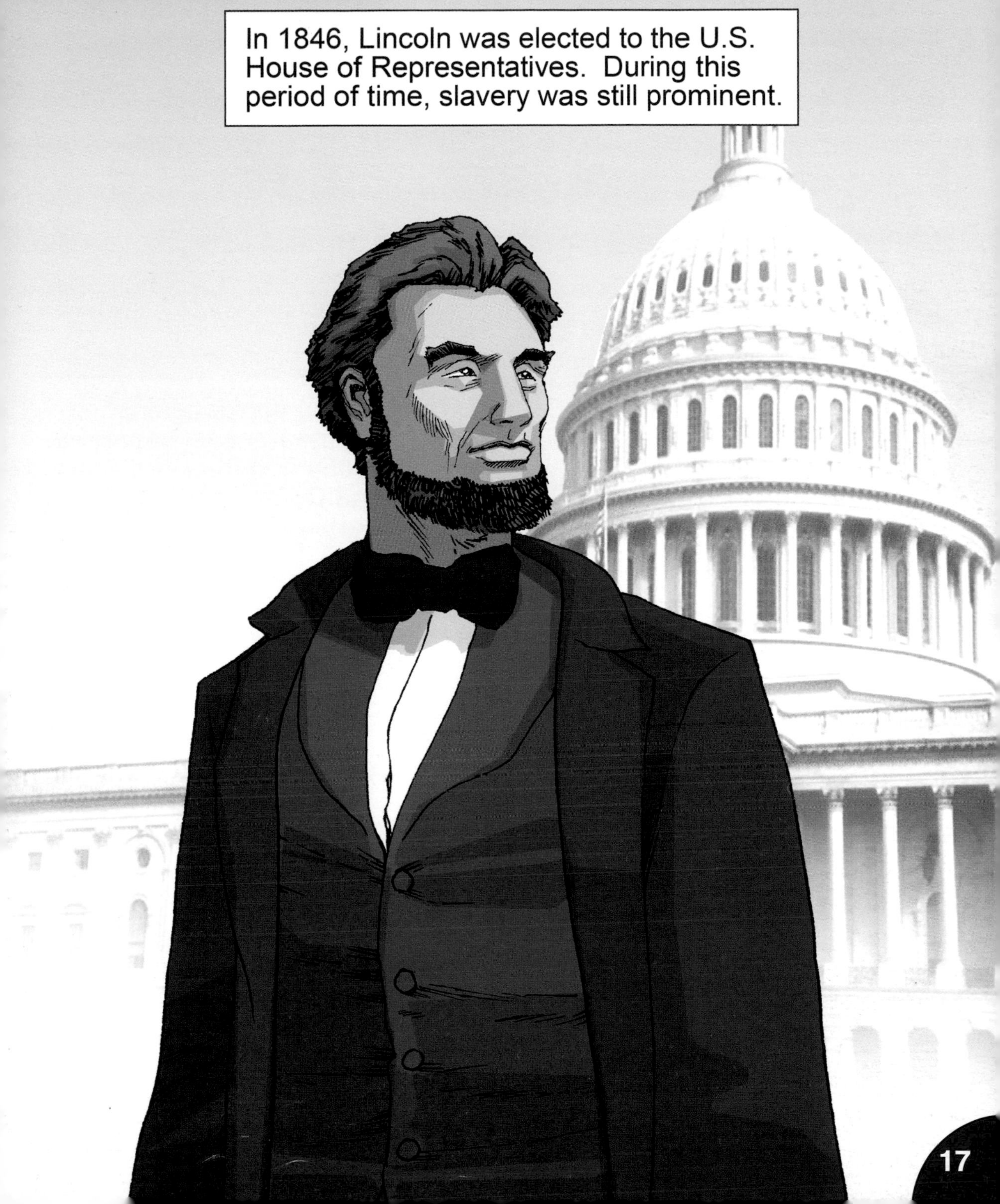
In 1846, Lincoln was elected to the U.S. House of Representatives. During this period of time, slavery was still prominent.

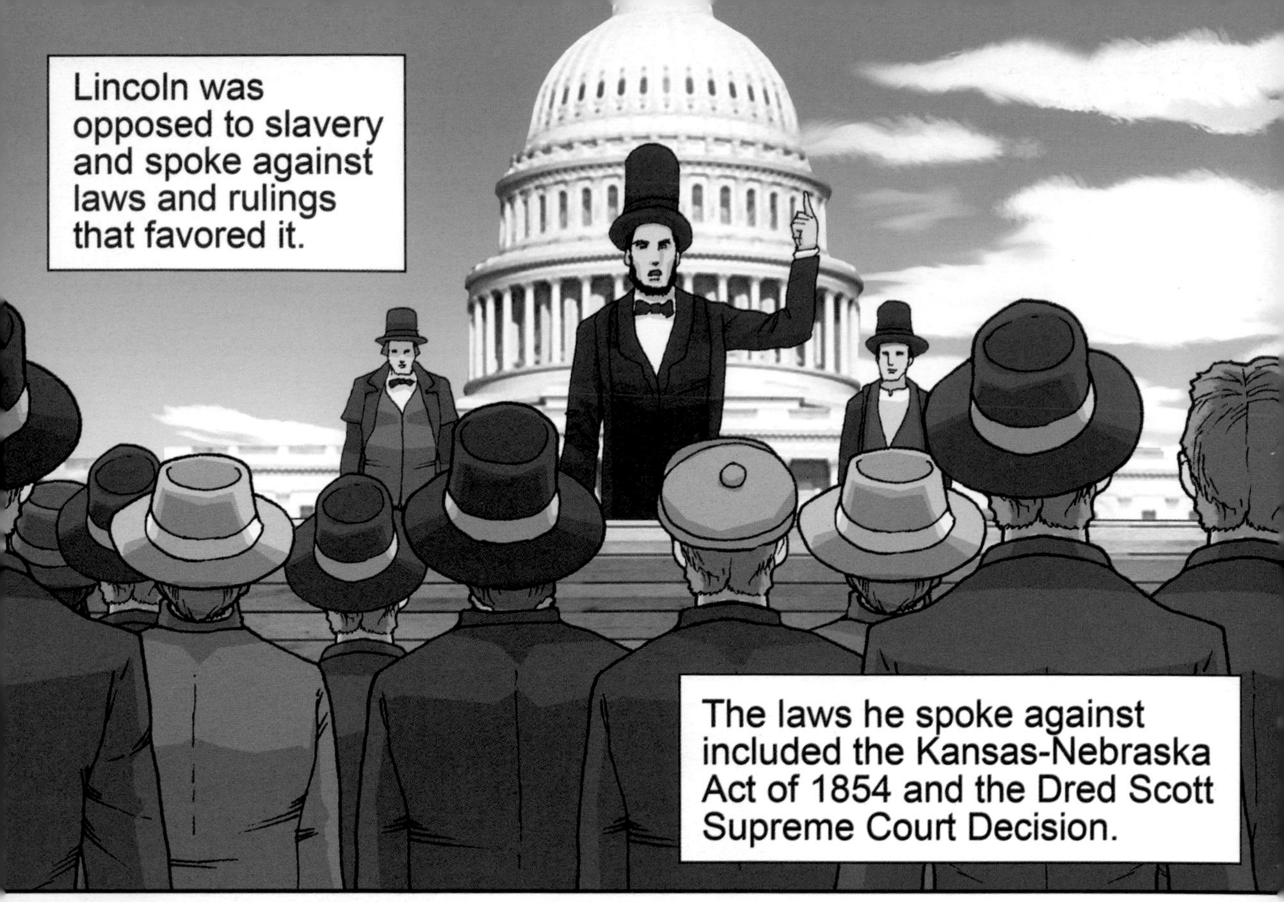
Lincoln was opposed to slavery and spoke against laws and rulings that favored it.
The laws he spoke against included the Kansas-Nebraska Act of 1854 and the Dred Scott Supreme Court Decision.

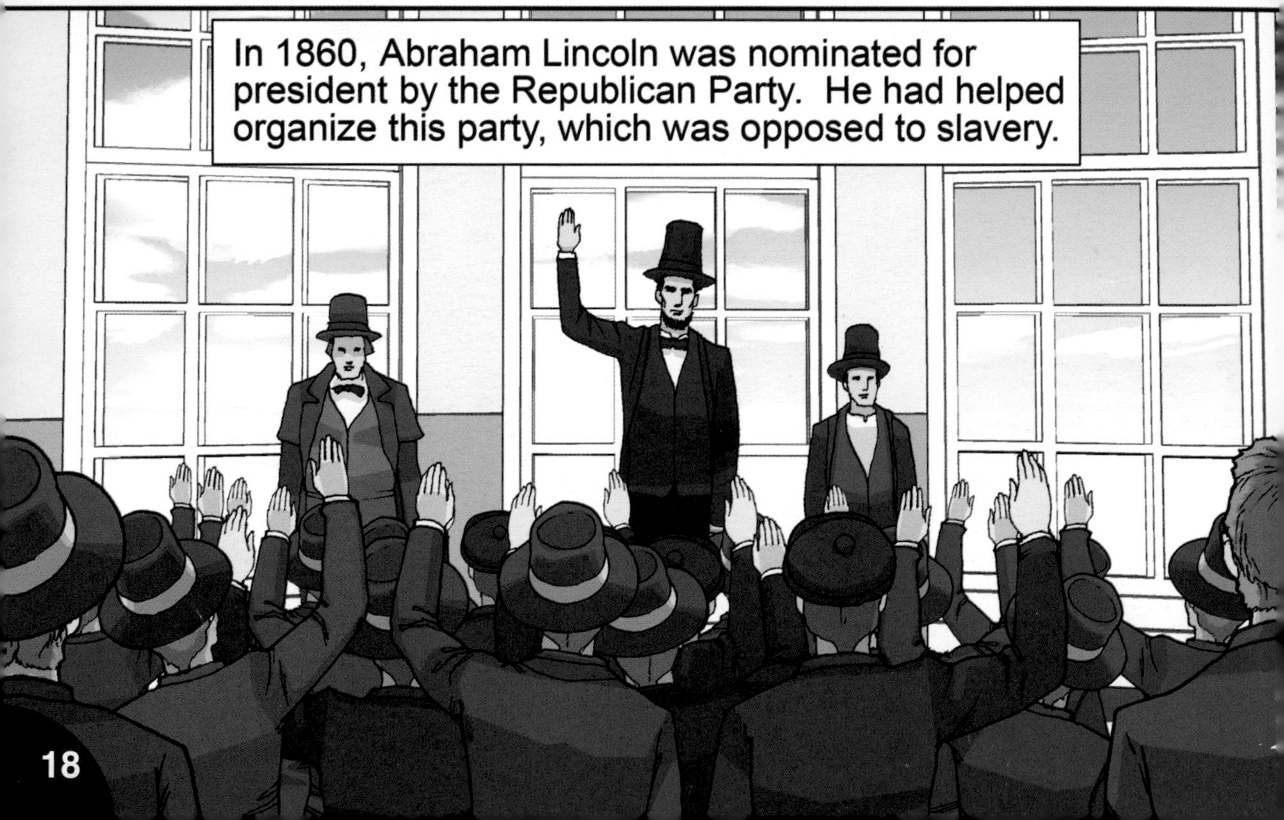
In 1860, Abraham Lincoln was nominated for president by the Republican Party. He had helped organize this party, which was opposed to slavery.

Chapter 6 President Abraham Lincoln

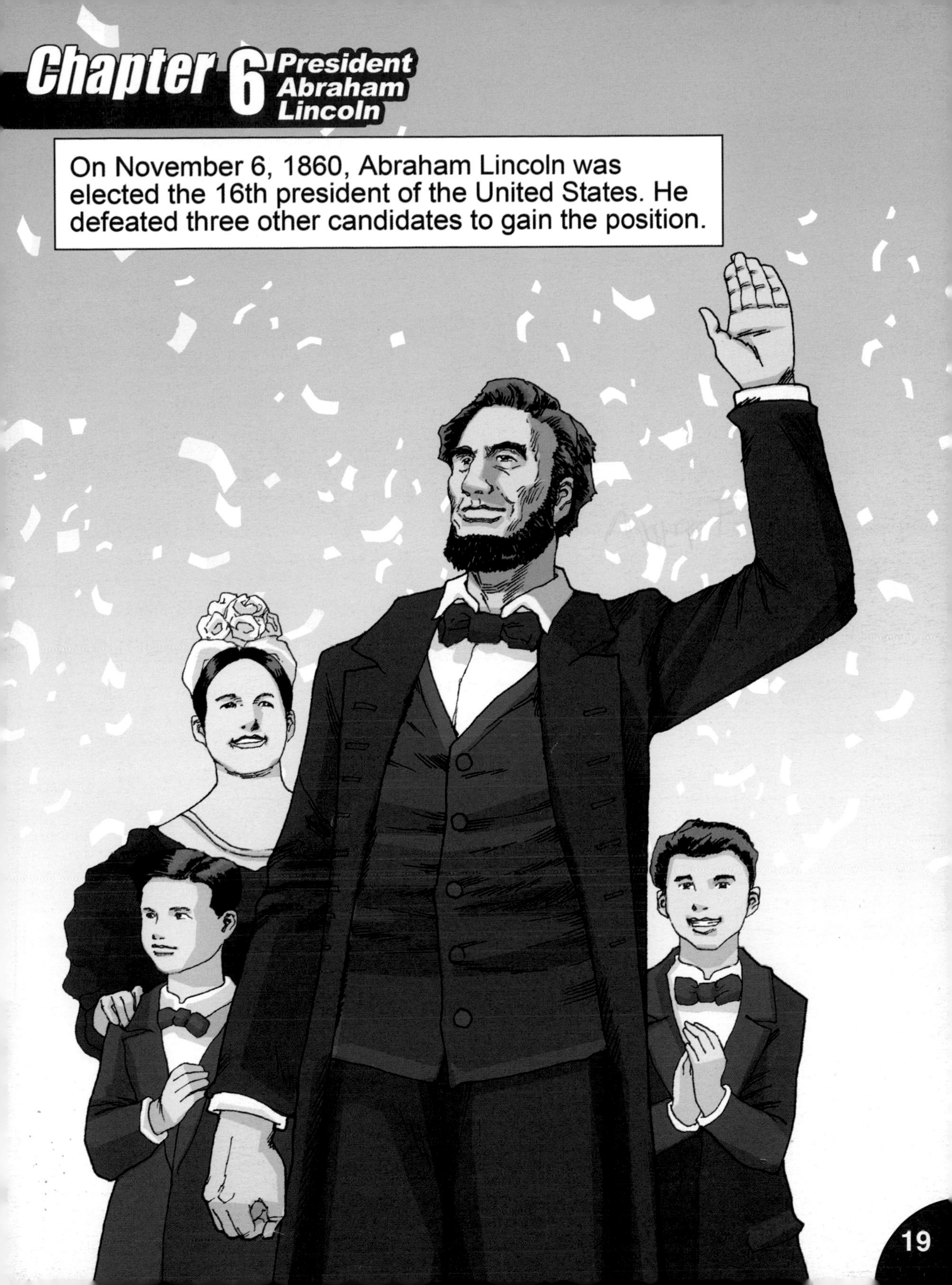
On November 6, 1860, Abraham Lincoln was elected the 16th president of the United States. He defeated three other candidates to gain the position.

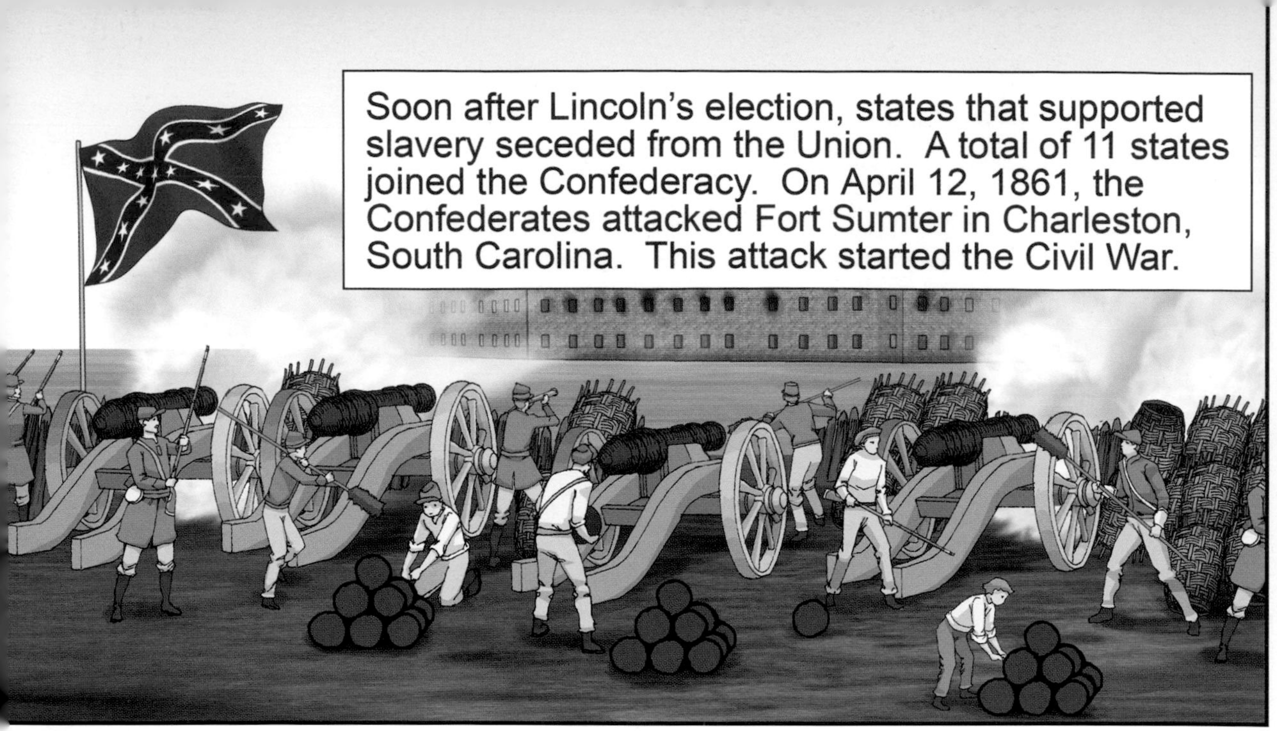
Soon after Lincoln's election, states that supported slavery seceded from the Union. A total of 11 states joined the Confederacy. On April 12, 1861, the Confederates attacked Fort Sumter in Charleston, South Carolina. This attack started the Civil War.

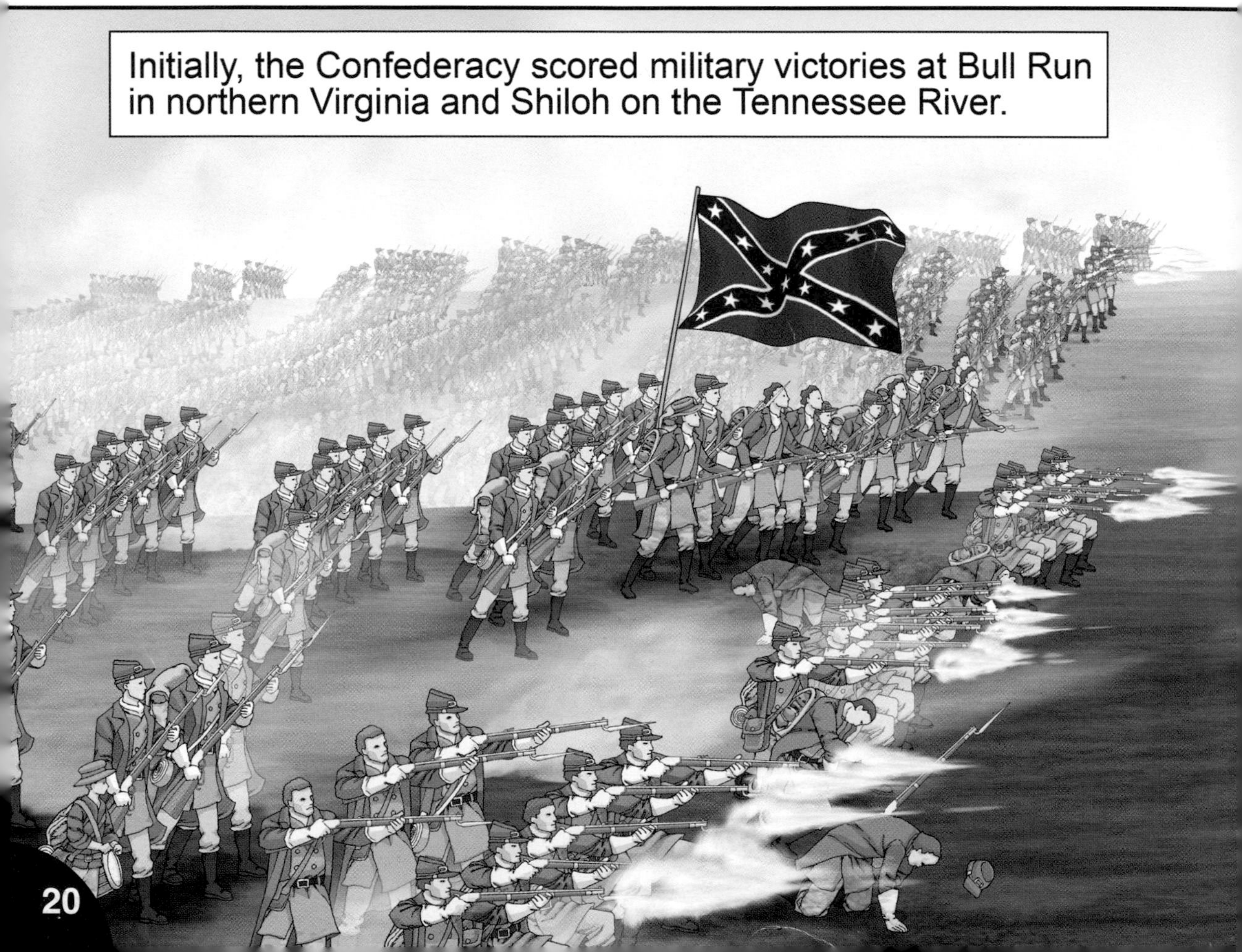
Initially, the Confederacy scored military victories at Bull Run in northern Virginia and Shiloh on the Tennessee River.

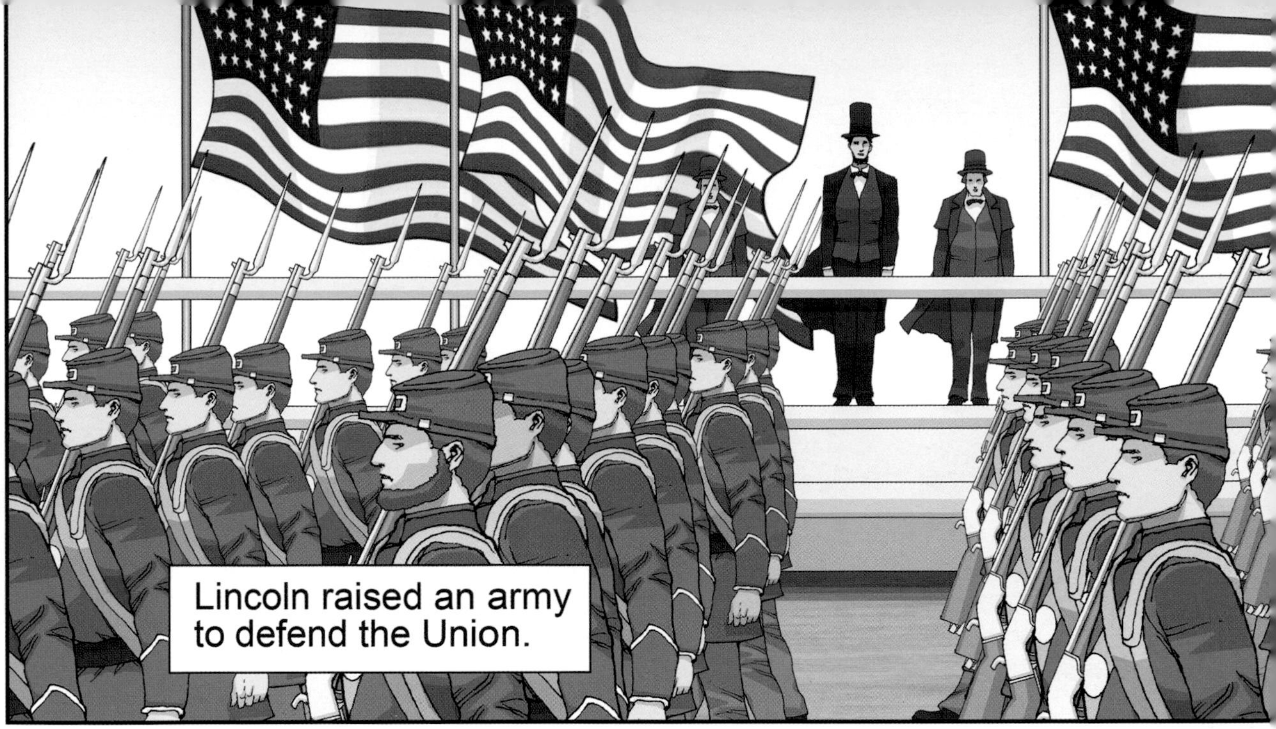
Lincoln raised an army
to defend the Union.

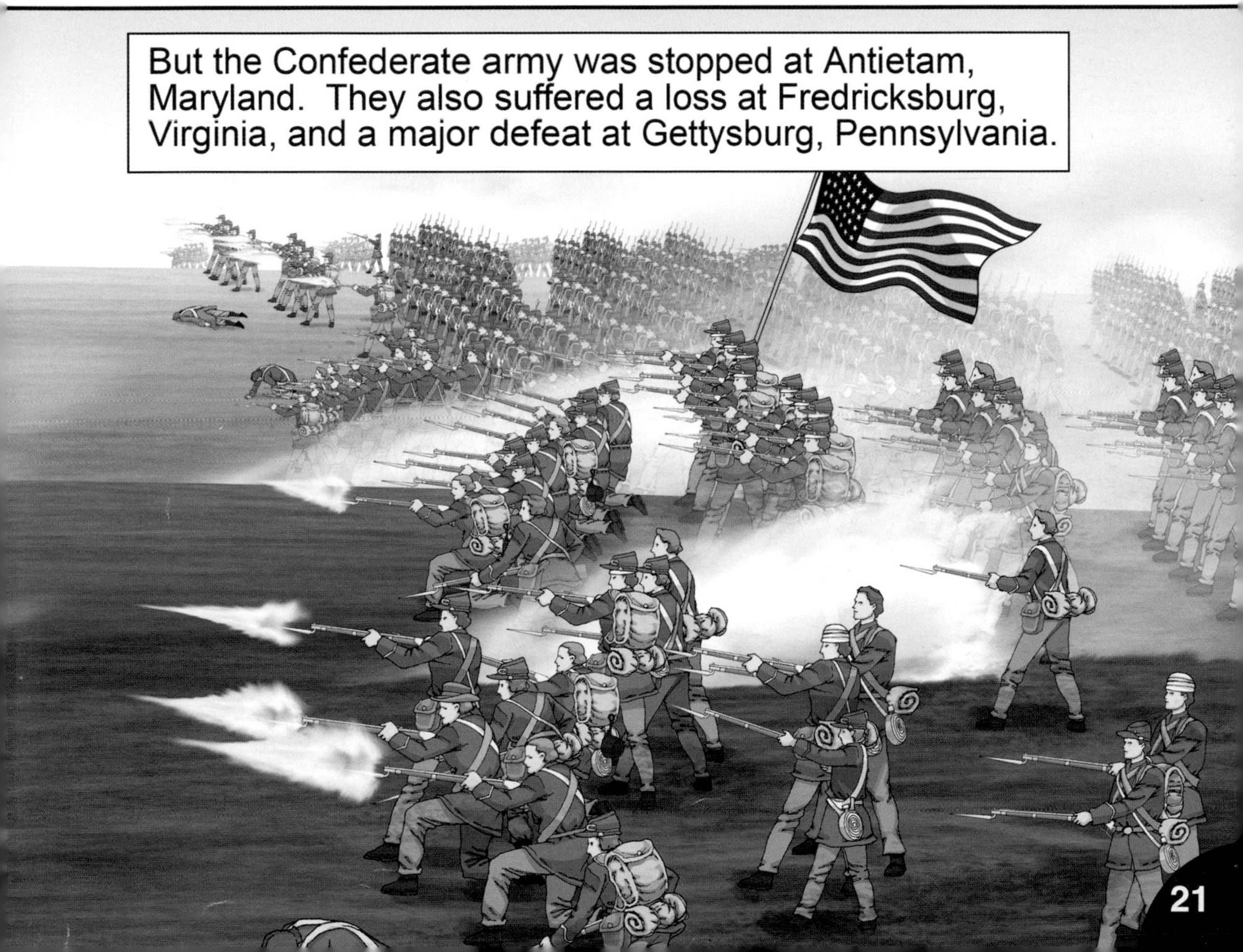
But the Confederate army was stopped at Antietam, Maryland. They also suffered a loss at Fredricksburg, Virginia, and a major defeat at Gettysburg, Pennsylvania.

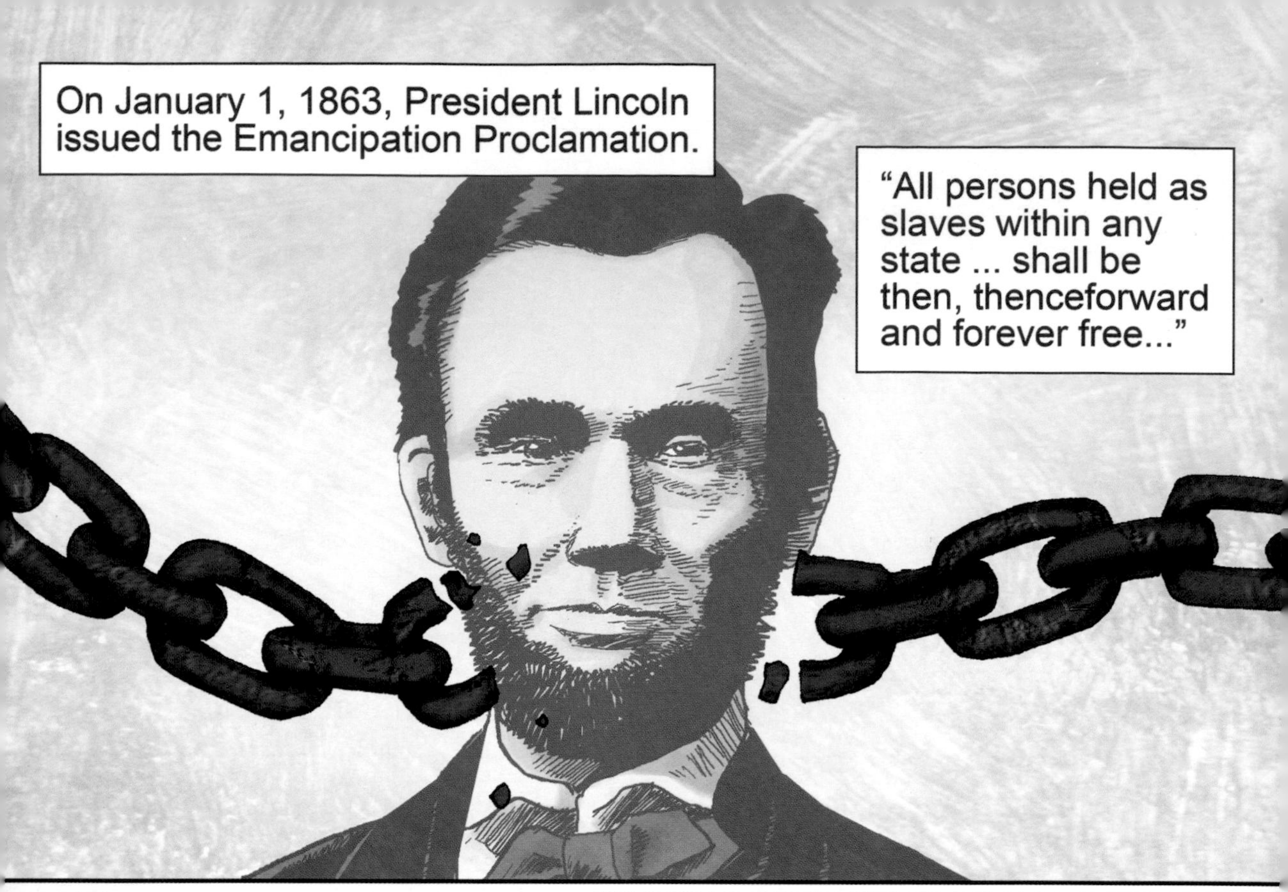
On January 1, 1863, President Lincoln issued the Emancipation Proclamation.
"All persons held as slaves within any state ... shall be then, thenceforward and forever free..."

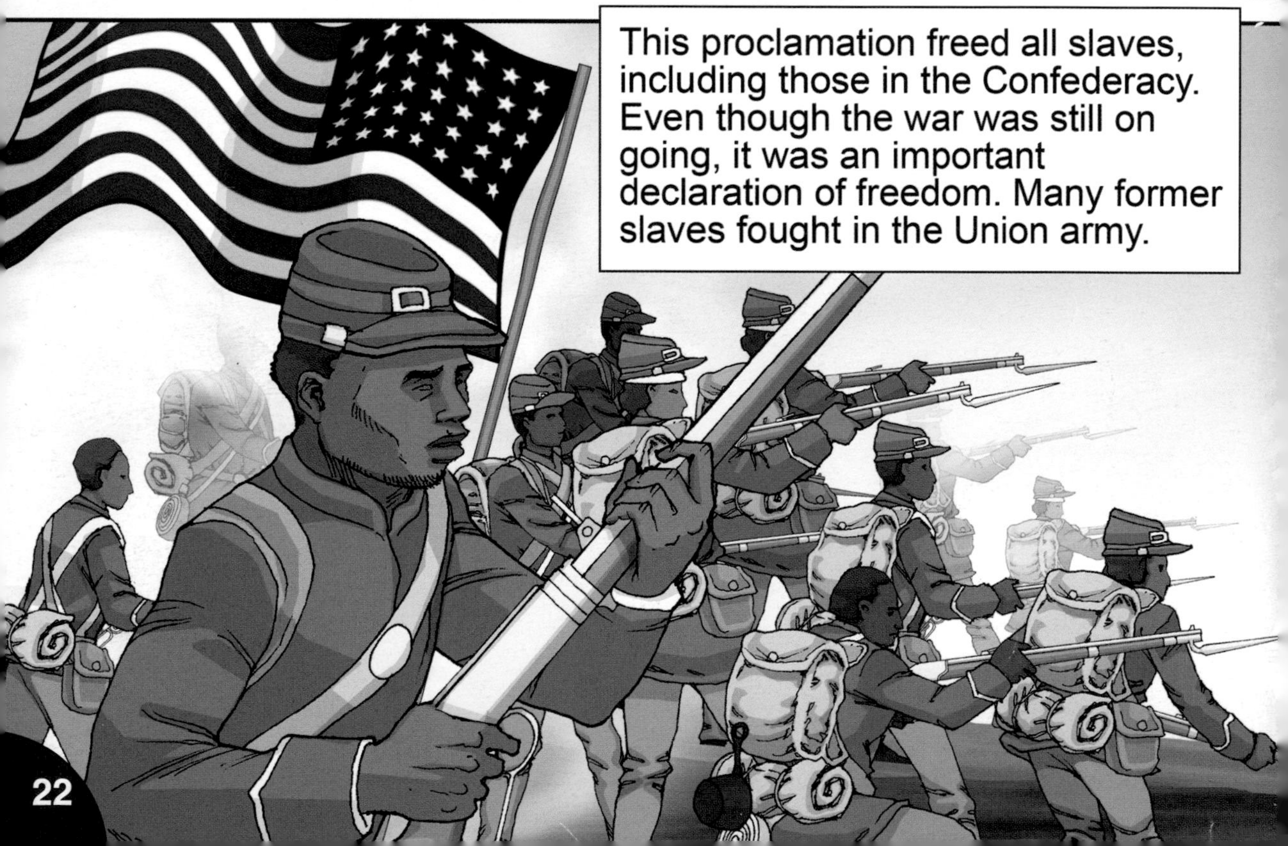
This proclamation freed all slaves, including those in the Confederacy. Even though the war was still on going, it was an important declaration of freedom. Many former slaves fought in the Union army.

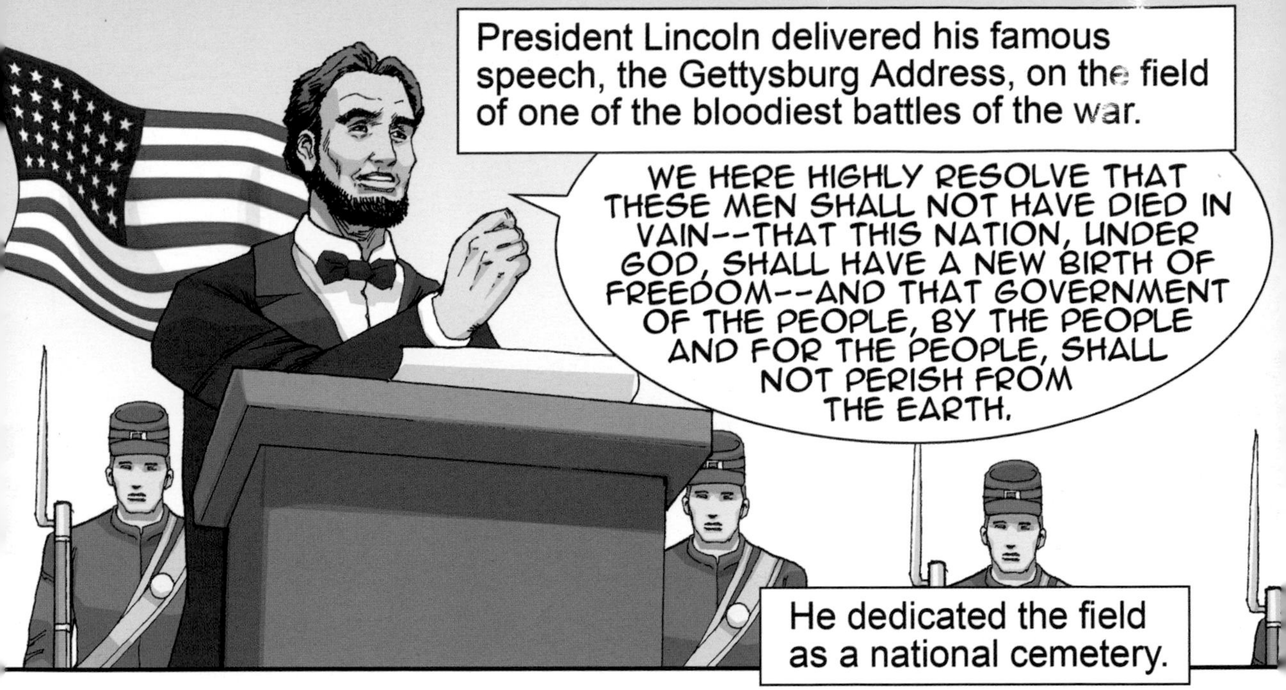
President Lincoln delivered his famous speech, the Gettysburg Address, on the field of one of the bloodiest battles of the war.
WE HERE HIGHLY RESOLVE THAT THESE MEN SHALL NOT HAVE DIED IN VAIN--THAT THIS NATION, UNDER GOD, SHALL HAVE A NEW BIRTH OF FREEDOM--AND THAT GOVERNMENT OF THE PEOPLE, BY THE PEOPLE AND FOR THE PEOPLE, SHALL NOT PERISH FROM THE EARTH.
He dedicated the field as a national cemetery.

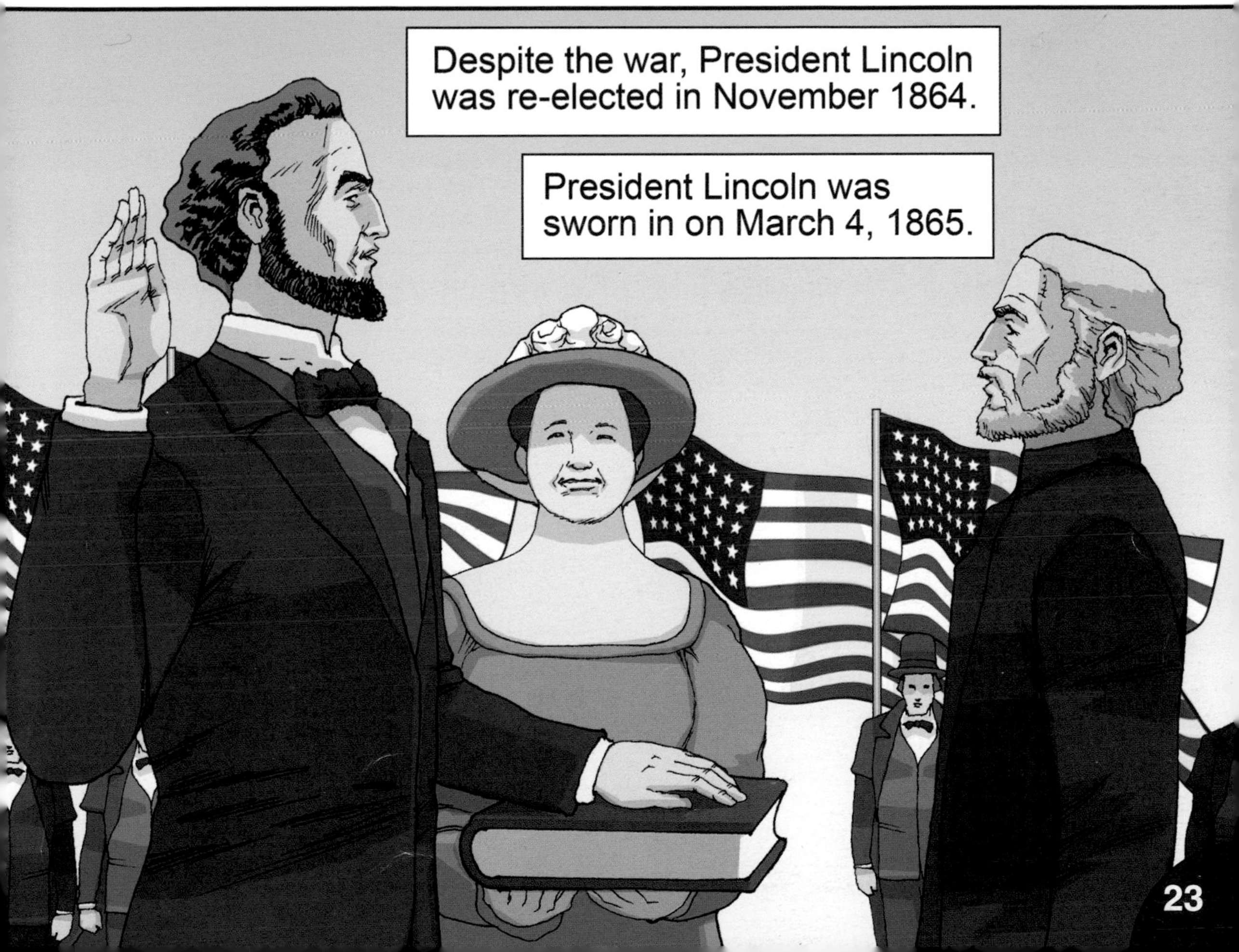
Despite the war, President Lincoln was re-elected in November 1864.
President Lincoln was sworn in on March 4, 1865.

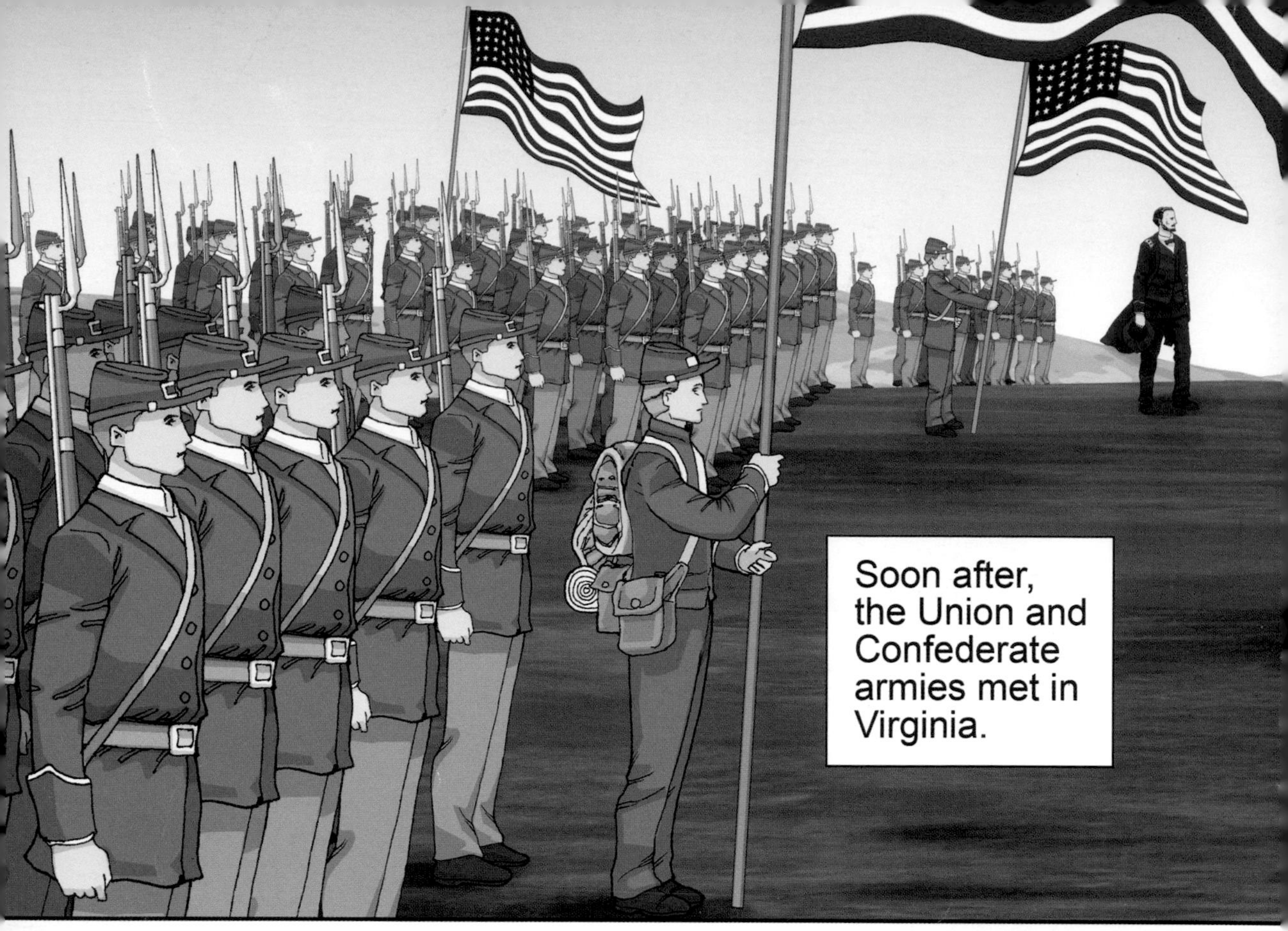
Soon after, the Union and Confederate armies met in Virginia.

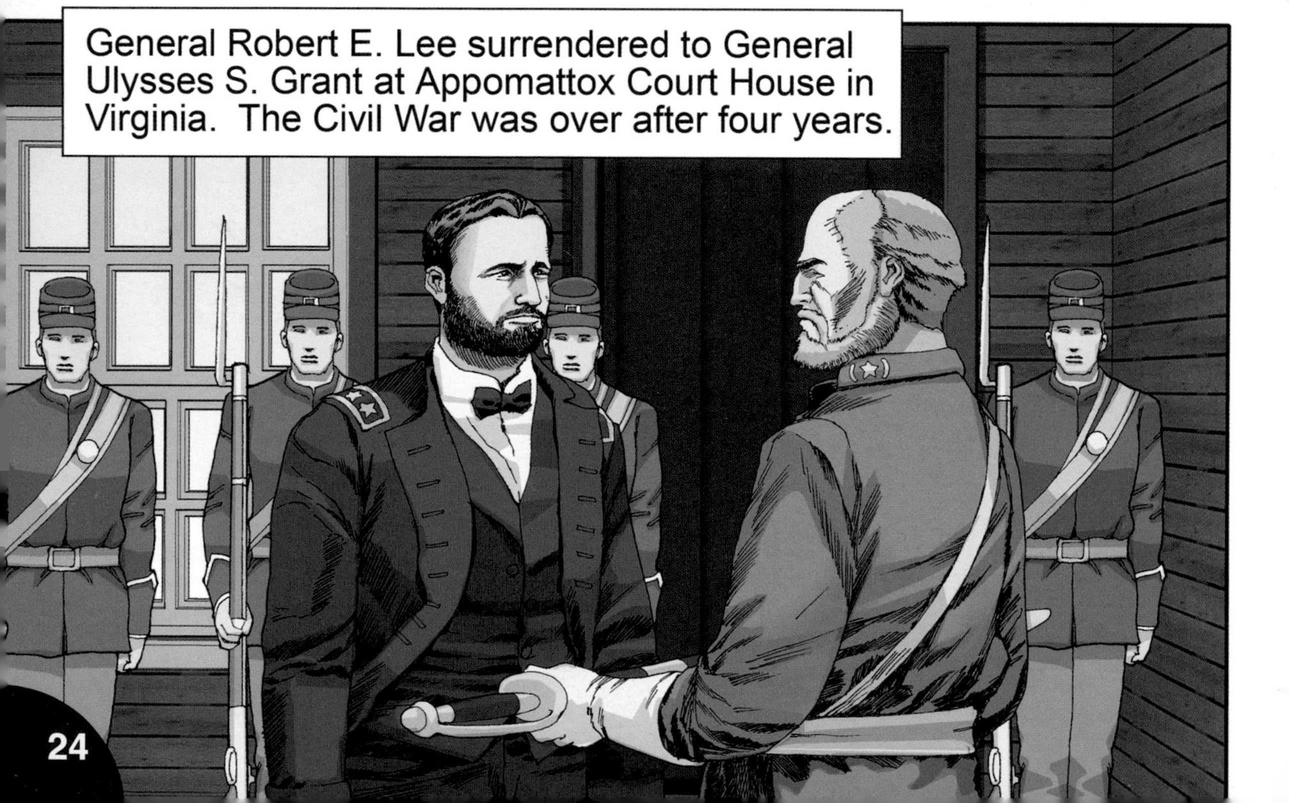
General Robert E. Lee surrendered to General Ulysses S. Grant at Appomattox Court House in Virginia. The Civil War was over after four years.

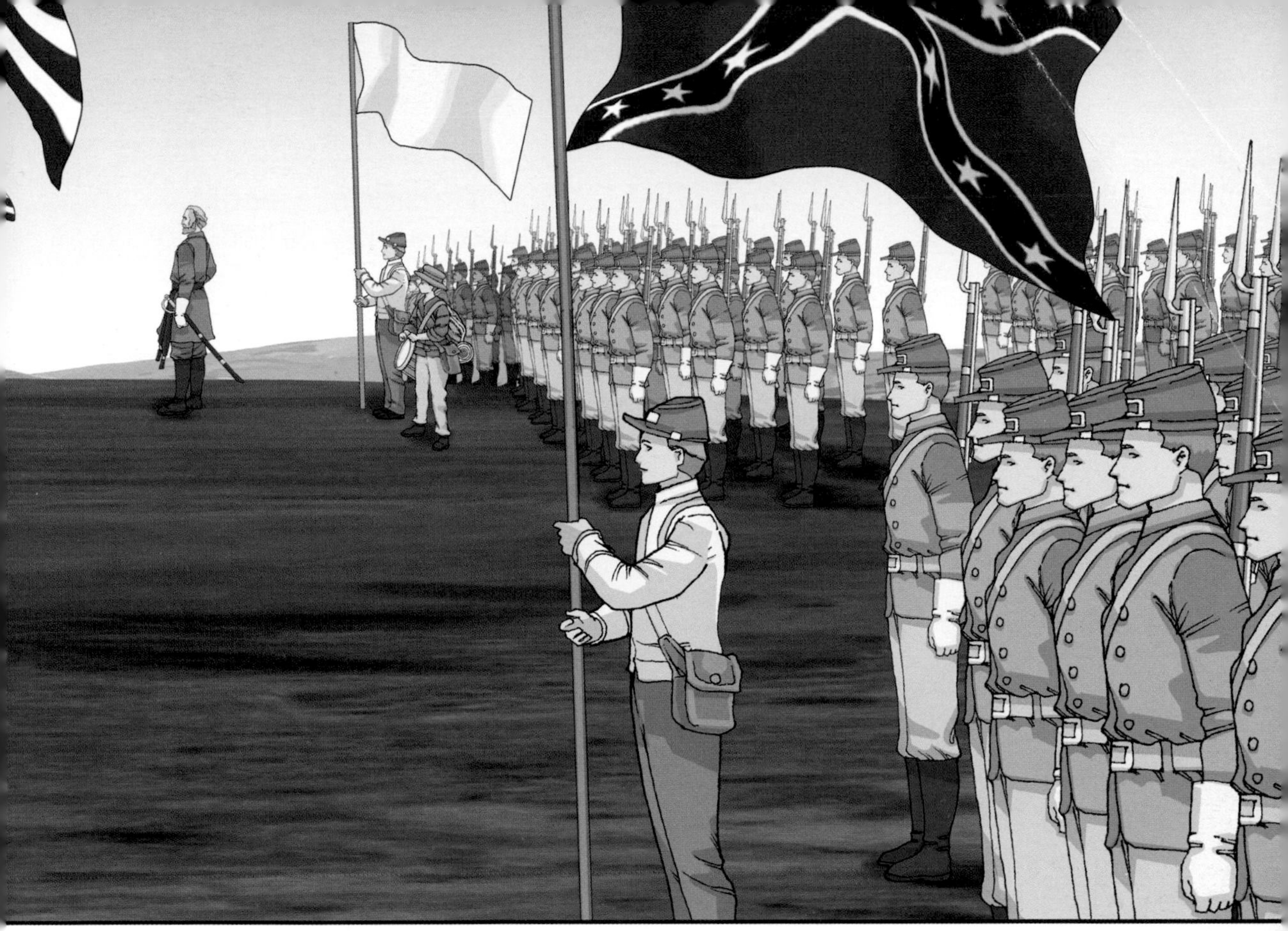

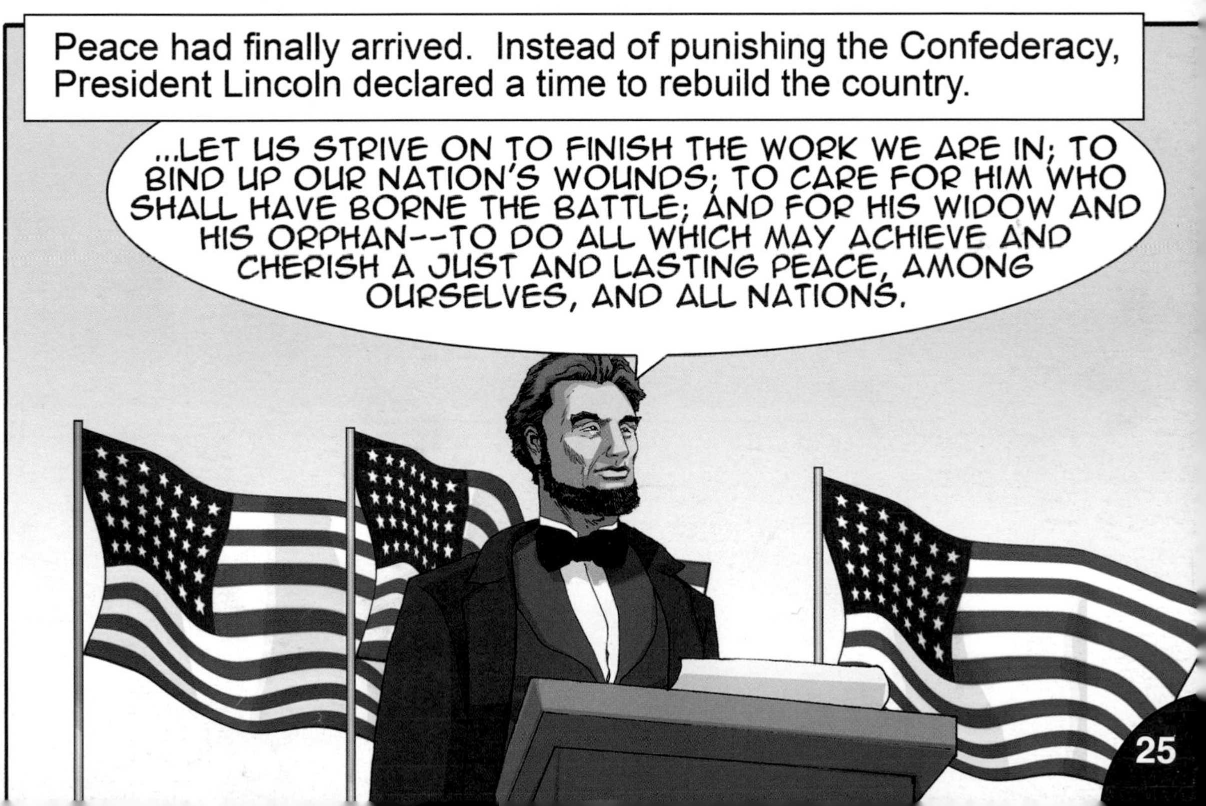
Peace had finally arrived. Instead of punishing the Confederacy, President Lincoln declared a time to rebuild the country.
...LET US STRIVE ON TO FINISH THE WORK WE ARE IN; TO BIND UP OUR NATION'S WOUNDS; TO CARE FOR HIM WHO SHALL HAVE BORNE THE BATTLE; AND FOR HIS WIDOW AND HIS ORPHAN--TO DO ALL WHICH MAY ACHIEVE AND CHERISH A JUST AND LASTING PEACE, AMONG OURSELVES, AND ALL NATIONS.

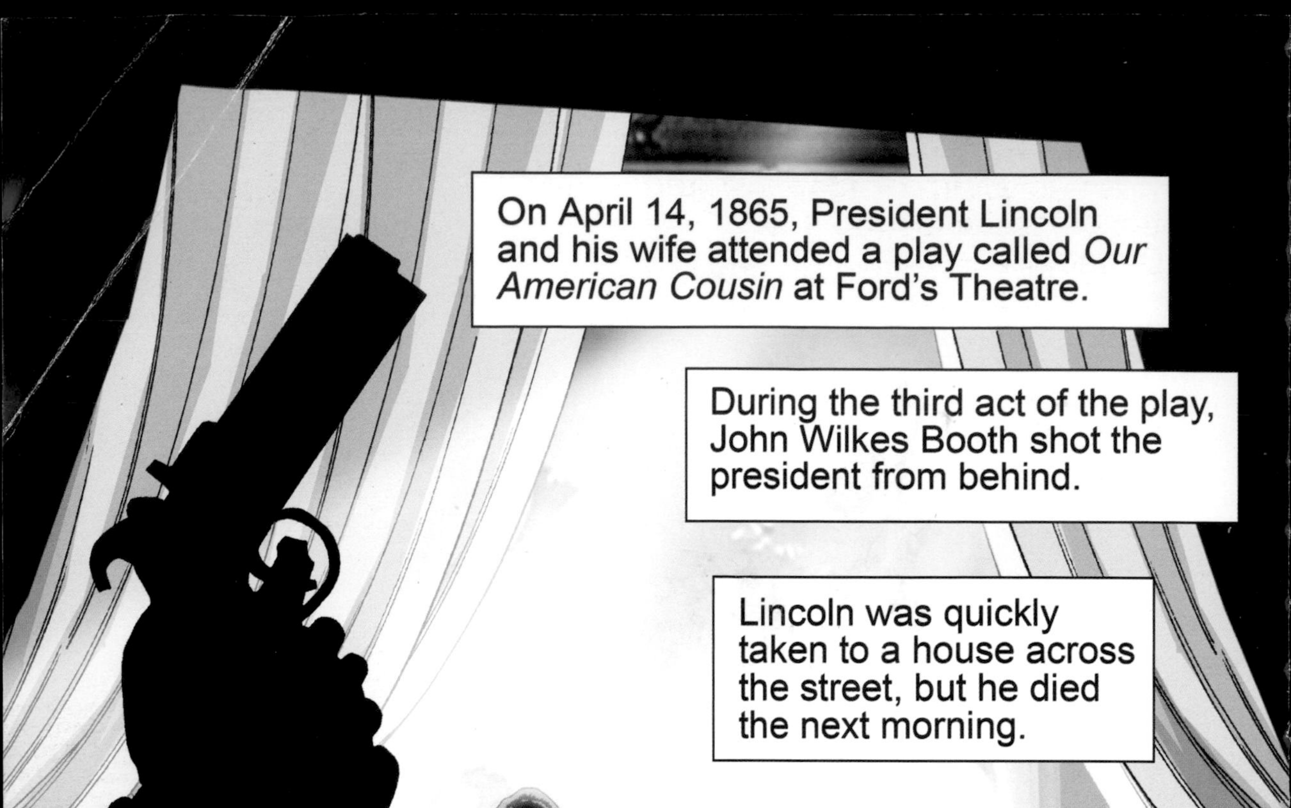
On April 14, 1865, President Lincoln and his wife attended a play called *Our American Cousin* at Ford's Theatre.
During the third act of the play, John Wilkes Booth shot the president from behind.
Lincoln was quickly taken to a house across the street, but he died the next morning.
John Wilkes Booth was cornered at a farm in Virginia. There, he was shot and killed.

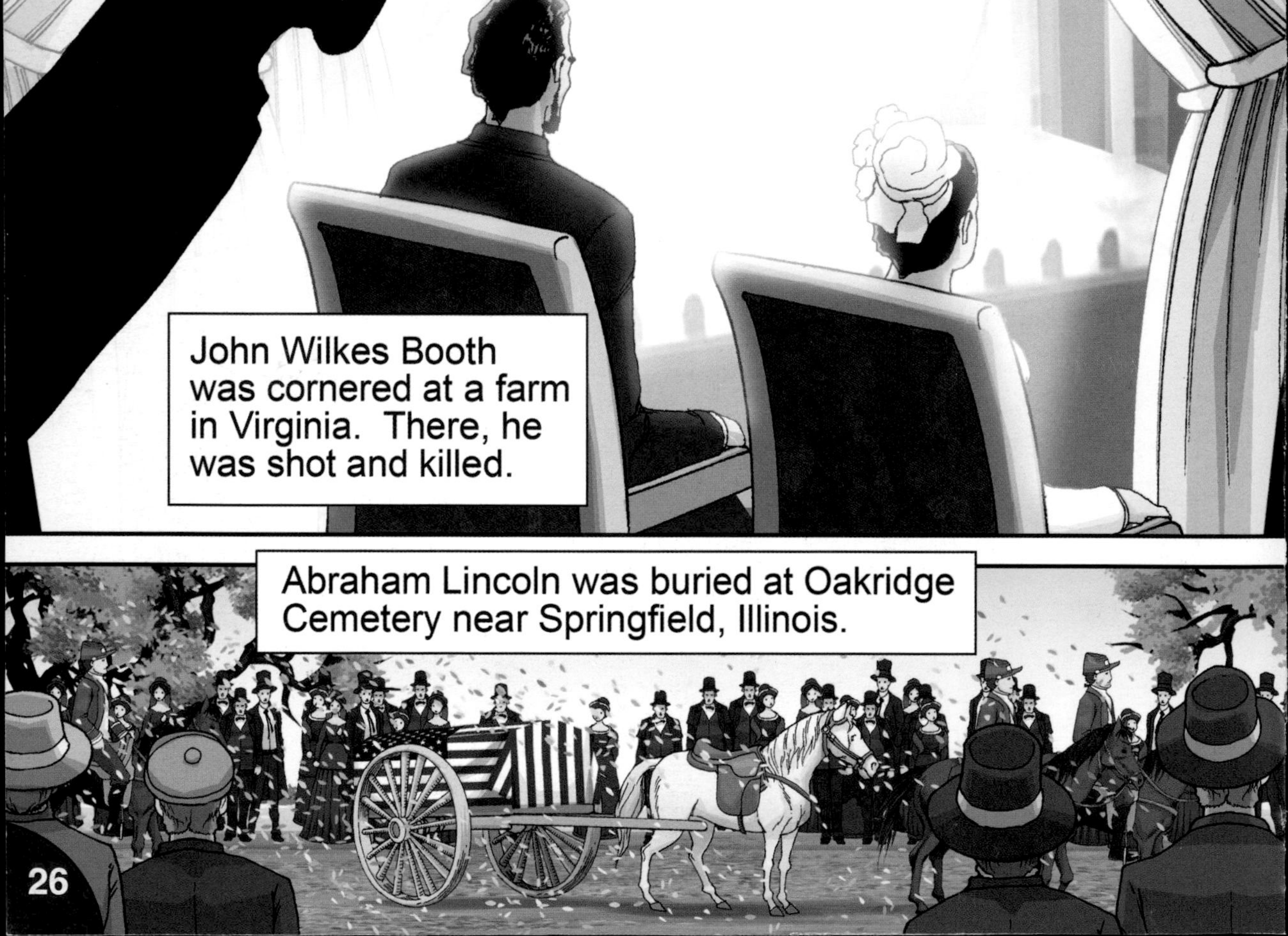
Abraham Lincoln was buried at Oakridge Cemetery near Springfield, Illinois.

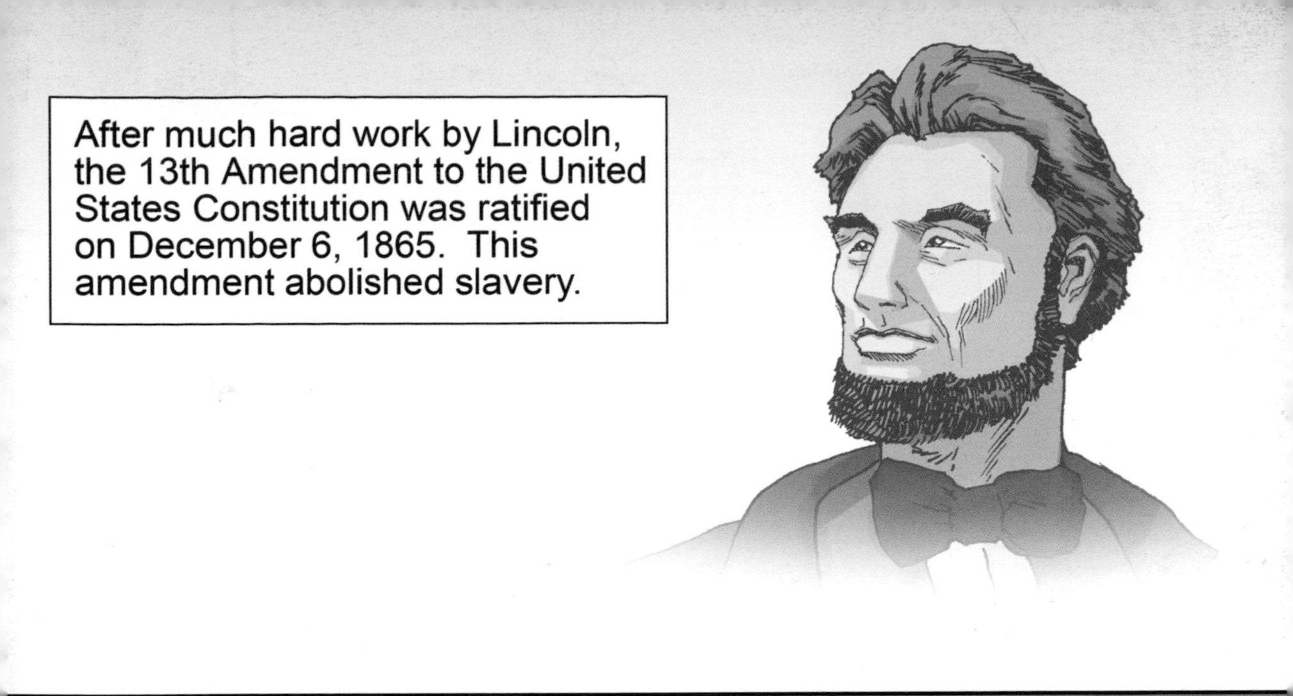
After much hard work by Lincoln, the 13th Amendment to the United States Constitution was ratified on December 6, 1865. This amendment abolished slavery.

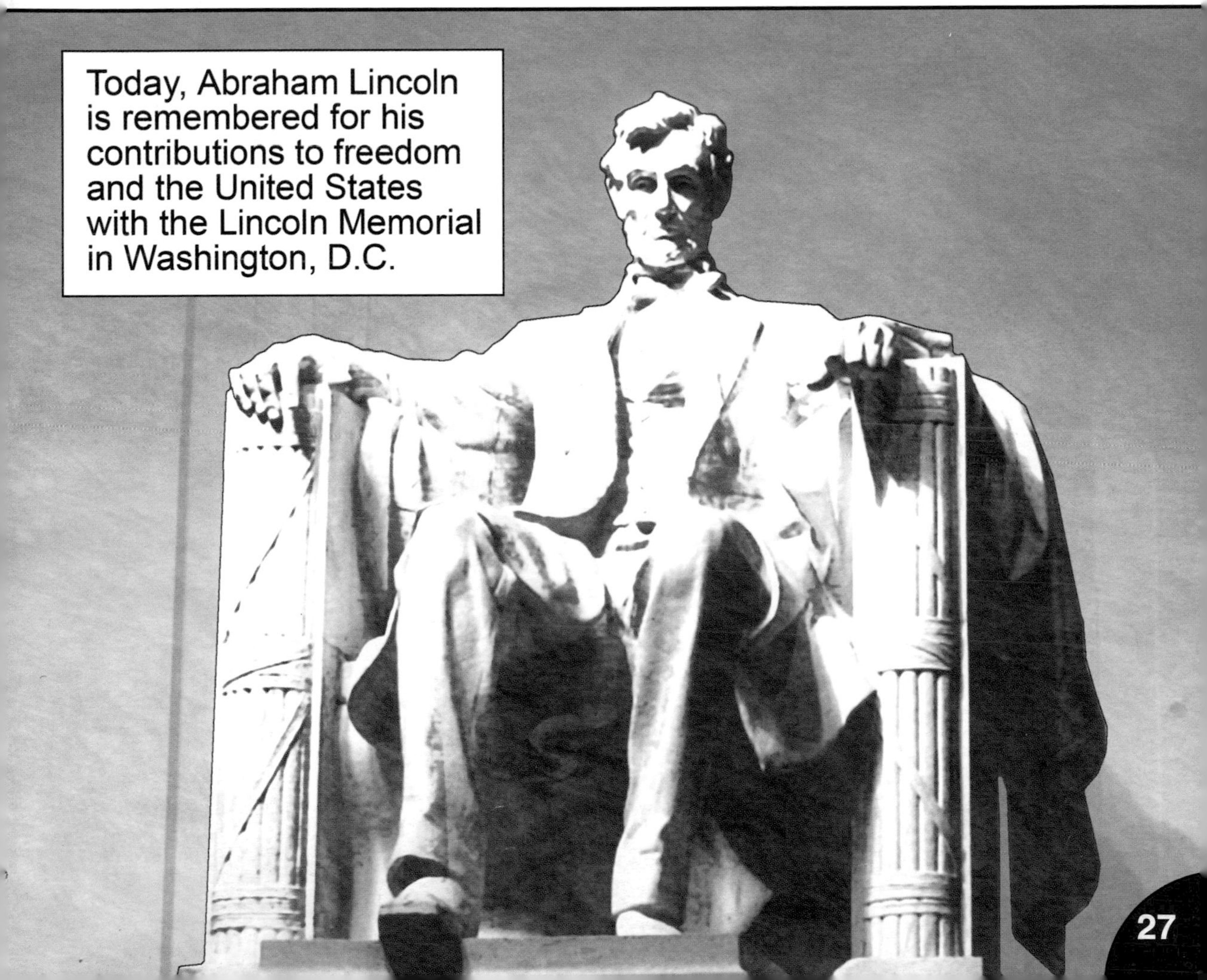
Today, Abraham Lincoln is remembered for his contributions to freedom and the United States with the Lincoln Memorial in Washington, D.C.

Timeline

February 12, 1809 - Abraham Lincoln was born in Kentucky.

1833 - Lincoln was appointed Postmaster and then Deputy Surveyor of New Salem.

August 4, 1834 - Lincoln was elected to the Illinois General Assembly.

November 4, 1842 - Lincoln married Mary Todd.

August 3, 1846 - Lincoln was elected to the U.S. House of Representatives.

November 6, 1860 - Lincoln was elected as the 16th President of the United States.

December 20, 1860 - Southern states started to secede from the Union.

April 12, 1861 - The Civil War began.

January 1, 1863 - Lincoln issued the Emancipation Proclamation, freeing all slaves.

November 19, 1863 - Lincoln delivered the Gettysburg Address.

November 8, 1864 - Lincoln was re-elected president.

April 9, 1865 - Lee surrendered to Grant at Appomattox Court House, ending the Civil War.

April 14, 1865 - While Lincoln was attending a play at Ford's Theater, John Wilkes Booth shot the President.

April 15, 1865 - President Lincoln died at 7:22 AM.

December 6, 1865 - The 13th Amendment passed, abolishing slavery.

UNITED STATES DURING THE AMERICAN CIVIL WAR

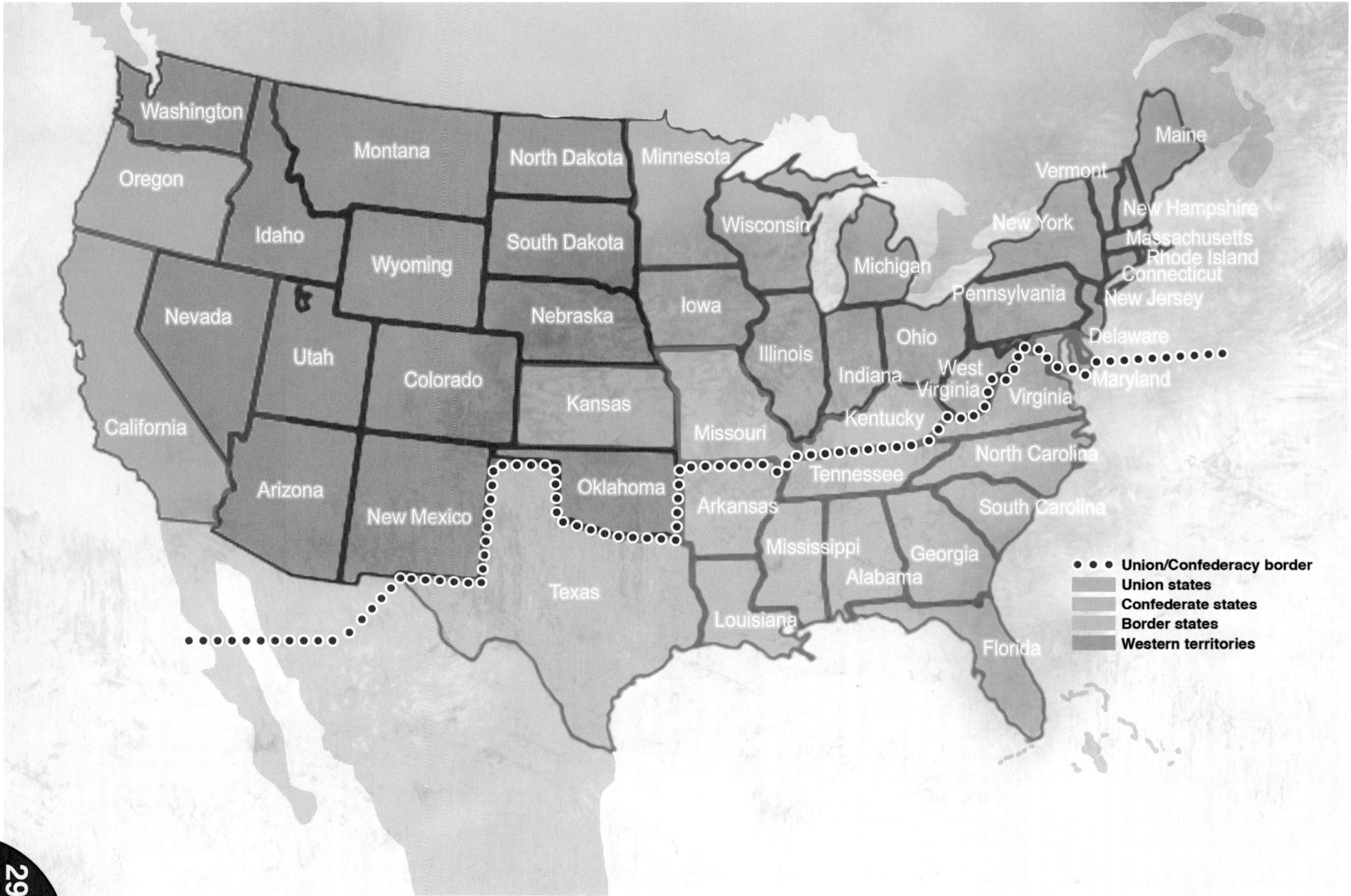
Washington
Oregon
California
Idaho
Nevada
Montana
Wyoming
Utah
Colorado
Arizona
New Mexico
North Dakota
South Dakota
Nebraska
Kansas
Oklahoma
Texas
Minnesota
Iowa
Missouri
Arkansas
Louisiana
Wisconsin
Illinois
Michigan
Indiana
Ohio
Kentucky
Tennessee
Mississippi
Alabama
Georgia
Florida
South Carolina
North Carolina
Virginia
West Virginia
Maryland
Delaware
Pennsylvania
New Jersey
New York
Connecticut
Rhode Island
Massachusetts
Vermont
New Hampshire
Maine
Union/Confederacy border
Union states
Confederate states
Border states
Western territories

Further Reading

Rivera, Sheila. *The Gettysburg Address*. American Moments. Edina: ABDO Publishing Company, 2004.

Venezia, Mike. *Abraham Lincoln*. New York: Scholastic Library Publishing, 2006.

Warycnia, Lou and Hale, Sarah Elder. *Abraham Lincoln: Defender of the Union*. Peterborough: Cobblestone Publishing, 2005.

Welsbacher, Anne. *Abraham Lincoln*. The United States Presidents. Edina: ABDO Publishing Company, 2001.

Glossary

amendment - a change to a country's constitution.

civil war - a war between groups in the same country. The United States of America and the Confederate States of America fought a civil war from 1861 to 1865.

Confederate States of America - the country formed by the states of South Carolina, Georgia, Florida, Alabama, Louisiana, Mississippi, Texas, Virginia, Tennessee, Arkansas, and North Carolina when they left the Union between 1860 and 1861. It is also called the Confederacy.

proclamation - an official public announcement.

ratify - to officially approve.

secede - to break away from a group.

Union - the states that remained in the United States during the Civil War.

Web Sites

To learn more about Abraham Lincoln, visit ABDO Publishing Company on the World Wide Web at **www.abdopublishing.com.** Web sites about Lincoln are featured on our Book Links page. These links are routinely monitored and updated to provide the most current information available.

Index